Praise for *Untapped Talent*

"Dani Monroe effectively combines research, case studies, storytelling, practical tools, and knowledge in this incredibly rich guide for recognizing and leveraging the untapped talent that surrounds us in business and in our everyday lives. *Untapped Talent* will be an invaluable resource for all who read it."

—Leslie Mays, VP, Global Diversity and Inclusion, Avon

"*Untapped Talent* is a refreshing read that provides extremely relevant ideas about how today's businesses need to pursue talent in all directions. This new thinking will change the game for businesses that sometimes struggle to engage a qualified and capable team."

—Mike Thompson, CEO, SVI

"If you are a company leader building a team and developing untapped talent, or, an individual trying to succeed on your own in corporate America, this insightful, engrossing, one-of-a kind book is perfect for you. The candid, compelling, real-life stories make the author's points in an entertaining and memorable way."

—Frank X. McCarthy, President, Diverse Workplace, Inc.

"Dani Monroe provides a voice of wisdom that rings unmistakably from a commitment to growing people, leaders, and organizations. The conversation about what it takes and the need to have solid global leaders is growing and is paramount in today's competitive market. Dani's insights into inclusion, talent engagement, and corporate culture lay a pragmatic and inviting path for anyone who wants to develop and grow their workforce."

—Amri Johnson, Director, Diversity & Inclusion, Novartis Institute Biomedical Research

This page intentionally left blank

Untapped Talent
Unleashing the Power of the Hidden Workforce

Dani Monroe

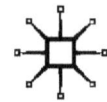

UNTAPPED TALENT
Copyright © Dani Monroe, 2013.
All rights reserved.

First published in 2013 by
PALGRAVE MACMILLAN®
in the United States—a division of St. Martin's Press LLC,
175 Fifth Avenue, New York, NY 10010.

Where this book is distributed in the UK, Europe and the rest of the world, this is by Palgrave Macmillan, a division of Macmillan Publishers Limited, registered in England, company number 785998, of Houndmills, Basingstoke, Hampshire RG21 6XS.

Palgrave Macmillan is the global academic imprint of the above companies and has companies and representatives throughout the world.

Palgrave® and Macmillan® are registered trademarks in the United States, the United Kingdom, Europe and other countries.

ISBN 978-1-349-44857-9   ISBN 978-1-137-32135-0 (eBook)
DOI 10.1057/9781137321350

Library of Congress Cataloging-in-Publication Data
Monroe, Dani.
    Untapped talent : unleashing the power of the hidden workforce / Dani Monroe.
        pages cm
    ISBN 978–1–137–28222–4 (alk. paper)
        1. Employee motivation. 2. Personnel management. 3. Leadership. I. Title.
HF5549.5.M63M656 2013
658.3'14—dc23   2012040609

A catalogue record of the book is available from the British Library.

Design by Newgen Imaging Systems (P) Ltd., Chennai, India.

First edition: April 2013

10 9 8 7 6 5 4 3 2 1

To my mother, Josephine, who taught me the heart of leadership; my father, Joseph, who broadened my horizon; and my husband, Steven, who supported me in "operating in purpose."

This page intentionally left blank

Contents

Acknowledgments	ix
Introduction: When Lightning Strikes	1

Part I Defining

Chapter 1	The Hidden Workforce	13
Chapter 2	Why Talent Goes Untapped	27
Chapter 3	Blame the Brain	43

Part II Mining and Refining

Chapter 4	Organizational Change: Tapping the 70 Percent	57
Chapter 5	The Culture Catapult	67
Chapter 6	The Serendipitous Soft Skills of Tapped Talent	85
Chapter 7	Personally Sound: Tapping into Your Talents	99

Part III Exemplifying

Chapter 8	The Three Rs: Emerging from the Hidden Workforce	117
Chapter 9	Seeing Solutions: The Role of Resourcefulness	125
Chapter 10	Failing Forward: The Role of Resilience	139
Chapter 11	Standing Firm: The Role of Resolve	151
Chapter 12	Tapped Talent: Putting Purpose on the Right Path	163

Notes	173
Index	177

This page intentionally left blank

Acknowledgments

Any new endeavor is always scary, exhilarating, and full of questions and learning. Questions about yourself, others, and what you're working on and how it will be received. Writing is an intimate process that one learns to trust overtime. It brings out the best of your inner thoughts and manages to raise the tension that resides within yourself between what you know, what you don't know, what you think you know, and what you will discover.

What I learned is that I'm not the same person I was one year ago this month when I started this journey. I have faced many fears along the way and slain some of my personal dragons. I've learned that to write a book is a community effort, even though you spend a lot of time alone deep in thought. Without encouragement, challenge, participation, and others' belief in me, *Untapped Talent: Unleashing the Power of the Hidden Workforce* may have never been written. For my immediate and larger community, a thousand thanks for just being present in my life. Especially my clients, that trusted my knowledge, skills and ability to guide them through transformative changes.

There are some in my community circle that need special attention for their special efforts. All my thanks and blessings to a person who was a stranger and became a true friend, Stephen Caldwell, an absolute genius with capturing your thoughts and translating them to the page. Stephen made me make sense, and together we created an incredible book. Thank you to Tommy Spaulding, a kindred spirit and bestselling author of *It's Not Who You Know*, for his introduction to Stephen, and to Mike Thompson, CEO of SVI, for his introduction to my agent, Herb Schaffner. Those four men connected the dots for me and laid the railroad tracks for my journey in becoming an author.

Thank you to The Partnership's Next Generation Executive Program and all my cohort group members that reminded me of the need for this book and became the final catalyst for getting it done. Deepest gratitude to the many volunteers who took time out to be interviewed and to tell their stories: Wayne Budd, Esq., Lisa Brooks Greaux ED, Mallik Angalakudati, Zaid Abdul-Aleem, Khadijah Abdulaleem, Denise Draper and Kim and Anne (whose names we changed). Plus others that shared parts of their stories but remain anonymous. Your generosity will serve to help millions operate in purpose.

They say good friends are there every step of the way, and mine really showed up. Debbie Anthony kept the cheerleading going when I was in doubt and in need of validation that I could achieve my dream. Monica Sturgis joined the support line with friendly phone calls that provided momentary relief. And Suzanne Owings shared guidance and insight when I got stuck and couldn't find the open door to the next paragraph or thought. To them, I owe my deepest gratitude.

I've been fortunate to have been surrounded by some of the best consulting minds in the country, and that circle added their expertise to the book: Richard Mansfield, PhD, researcher; Tim Ewing, PhD, reviewer; Amri Johnson, director of Diversity at Novartis Institute of Biomedical Research; and Dr. Price Cobbs for seeing my talent in the early years and putting it into play.

Thanks also to my fabulous Middlesex County Chapter Link's Sisters, who kept me focused and on task, especially Dorothy Terrell, president, and Jackie Glenn, member, and the vice president of Diversity & Inclusion, EMC2, who lent their endorsements during the critical book proposal phase. Their endorsements were joined by Law Burks, VP and General Manager, Illinois Tool Works, Inc., and Stanley G. Eakins, the dean of East Carolina University's College of Business.

A good editor is worth her weight in gold, and Laurie Harting sharpened my thoughts and saved me from myself on many occasions during the writing process.

A lifelong thanks to my brother, Robert Perkins, and my sisters, Valencia Wright, Joanne Lee, and Cherry Goudeau, for protecting me during my development years and nurturing me as only big brothers and big sisters can, with unconditional love. And to my children, Shirrona, Karima, Willie, and Serena, who provided inspiration to write the book and have taught me so much about learning to appreciate others' talent.

A heartfelt thanks to my husband, Steven H. Wright, for his patience, support, and love as I disappeared into myself to answer my call. I stand taller because of you.

In gratitude to all!

This page intentionally left blank

Introduction: When Lightning Strikes

This page intentionally left blank

Electricity is really just organized lightning.
—George Carlin, comedian

The epiphany came in stages, which, when you think about it, isn't unusual. Epiphanies, by definition, come with a flash, but that lightning-strike moment of clarity almost always develops in a storm that starts with a single cloud and builds over time.

So in 1983—in my thirties, fresh out of graduate school, and primed to launch a career in organizational development—an innocent-looking wisp of a cloud drifted along the horizon of my life. It came in the form of a magazine article featuring Dr. Price Cobbs, the famed psychiatrist, author, and consultant based in San Francisco, California. Little did I know that it would put me on a course of discovery about untapped talents—in myself and in others.

Dr. Cobbs shook the world considerably in 1968 when he coauthored *Black Rage*, with William H. Grier, MD, one of the first books on the mental health of African Americans.[1] It provided a revealing, painful portrait of the suppressed anger and frustration felt by millions of people still struggling to find their fit in society roughly one hundred years after Generals Lee and Grant convened at the Appomattox Court House to end the Civil War. The book also established Dr. Cobbs as a pioneering authority on what's come to be known as "diversity and inclusion" in the workplace. He founded Pacific Management Systems in 1967, stopped seeing patients, and focused his energies on executive development and consulting that helped individuals and organizations address the realities identified in his books.

I'm still not entirely certain why Dr. Cobbs's work struck a chord with me. My understanding of race and racial issues was very limited at the time. I grew up in a family that identified culturally with African Americans; but, in reality, we were a multicultural stew cooked in its own little melting pot of spices. An African American man and his white Jewish wife produced the offspring known as my father, Joseph Sharfter Perkins. And Josephine Williams, my light-skinned mother, was Creole, that hard-to-define people group that originated with French, Spanish, and black settlers and grew to include just about anyone in southern Louisiana who "mixed" with them. Together, Joseph and Josephine raised eight children with skin hues as different as the paints my dad mixed to brush on the walls of the houses on California's Monterey Peninsula.

I was the youngest and the only one with a college degree. My plans, quite simply, were to change the world. But I'd never considered working in diversity and inclusion. As I mentioned, that phrase hadn't even been coined. So after finishing Pepperdine's organizational development program in 1983, I looked for work as a consultant on large system change projects. I wanted to help businesses on issues pertaining to mergers and acquisitions, downsizing/rightsizing, organization transitions, and leadership development.

That's when I came across a *Black Enterprise* article in which Dr. Cobbs talked about how African Americans and Latinos could grow as leaders in American corporations. It moved me so deeply that I picked up the phone and called him.

Our initial conversation led to a face-to-face meeting at his office in San Francisco, and six months later my focus on generic organizational change had, well, changed. Suzanne Owings, a change consultant who at the time was a project and organization planner with the Bechtel Group, had given me some valuable advice about finding the focus for my consulting practice: "Don't define your practice," she said. "Let your work define your specialty. It will emerge from the work you do." And it did. I joined Dr. Cobbs's team, and my work began to define my specialty. My work soon connected two very important components of my life: my interests and experiences in organizational development and my identity as a person of color.

Looking back, I realize that my race consciousness was always there; it's just that it was hiding below the surface. How could it not have been there, coming from mixed-race parents with features that were questioned by both blacks and whites?

Race was and is a part of my everyday life; but it didn't and doesn't define my total life experience or worldview, which are varied and influenced by myriad events, situations, and people. The total sum of my existence allows me to exercise emotional elasticity—the ability to travel through different spaces in life.

My work through the years has helped me discover how the various factors that define each of us shape our talents, the use of our talents, the talents of the people we lead, and the use of the talents of the people we lead. Those factors shape the potential within us all, as well as how (or if) we will realize that potential.

My first memorable experience with this reality came during one of my initial assignments—a five-day leadership development course for African Americans. I had worked with nonprofits and in education, but never directly with a corporate audience. What struck me with great clarity—the epiphany that had been building among the clouds in the months since I first read the article featuring Dr. Cobbs—was the amount of undervalued and underdeveloped talent sitting in the room during that seminar.

Over the course of my career, I saw hundreds of extremely intelligent, well-credentialed men and women with master's degrees in business, degrees in engineering, math, technology, and liberal arts. They all had a strong desire to succeed in their work, but they all faced unique organizational obstacles. For a variety of reasons, many of which it took me years to uncover and understand, these professionals represented silenced voices in their workplaces. They represented what I've now come to define as "untapped talent"—professionals with relevant skills and abilities who aren't making the most of them.

These are professionals who aren't given the opportunities to use and grow their skills and abilities. Or they have been promoted but then experience resistance to their ideas and solutions from their managers and peers. Or they are marginalized—they have the position but not the authority to accomplish business goals. Or they experience what I call "work-a-rounds." They are on a team but other people spend more time working around them than interacting with them directly. So it takes extra time and energy for the team to succeed. They are politely ignored until they're transferred to another assignment. Or they are professionals who aren't showing the personal responsibility and initiative for driving their career forward.

When I looked at that room full of professionals at that leadership conference, I saw a room full of untapped talent. It's not that they were unsuccessful or that they weren't using their talents; it's just that most of them were falling far shy of their potential. Some may not have been fully aware of all their talents, much less how to put them to use in their work environments. While the work environment can and does challenge our success, we also have a responsibility to manage and advocate for our careers. Many of these professionals were ineffective when it came to knowing how best to manage their potential.

Even if they recognized their untapped talents and adopted the right mindsets for advancing their careers, they still had to return to environments that didn't foster that development—and sometimes worked against it. Even the best-intentioned managers struggled to recognize their unique talents and develop them.

Good intentions alone weren't sufficient to build the skills necessary for success in corporate cultures that were immune to differences. Good intentions can manifest in weak policy statements or in soft hiring and promotion goals that offer no real direction to the manager and keep untapped talent questioning the corporation's commitment to advancement and development.

How many of you have a hiring goal that sounds something like this: "One out of four of our candidates will come from diverse backgrounds"? If so, then you may be operating under the assumption that "inclusion" in the screening process leads to diverse hires. This typically isn't true, for reasons that we'll discuss in later chapters. Instead, what you've accomplished is the ability to say you were "fair."

My experiences in that leadership development course started a 30-year journey of running leadership labs for African Americans, women, Latinos, and other groups that, for one reason or another, were considered "diverse." I also worked with executives at the highest levels, from regional banks to global pharmaceutical giants to the intelligence industry to technology organizations to medical agencies. And I continued to see the same caliber of bright, high-desire people who struggled or had struggled to succeed in their work environments. Some of them shattered the glass ceiling and became very successful; others maintained the status quo and didn't grow to their potential, never hitting that peak performance level. Some tapped into their talents early in life and never stopped, and we can learn from those leaders. Others tapped into it for a while, then stalled—at mid-management or near the top of the organization chart.

As you read through these pages, keep in mind that untapped talent can exist at any level of the organization—even at the top. Talent can be silenced with political dynamics, changes in leadership or reorganization, or any number of other factors. We've all had the experience of being confined in a role and having to compromise our ideas and concepts to meet our managers' objectives. Deep inside we knew the results of our work or our presentation would only address 50 percent of the problem. We shrank inside while going through the motions of supporting the boss and the organization. If this has happened to you, then congratulations, you experienced untapped talent.

I've also discovered that untapped talent comes in many different forms. Diversity, in other words, is quite diverse. Most people never hit their talent ceilings, and that reality isn't exclusive to any race or gender. We all muddle along at times, wrestling with the discomfort that growth brings. It's too often easier to stand still and do nothing than to go and grow.

The factors that shape the talents that so often go "untapped" are varied and complex, so untapped talents can, and pretty much do, exist in everyone. It can be the white male who went to a small state college and is trying to thrive in a corporation that sees only Ivy Leaguers as leaders. It can be the woman with children who finds that others make decisions about her ability to take on assignments or positions that require travel. It can be the 50-something-year-old ex-Marine who is seen as old and overly rigid in a corporate culture that believes innovation comes only by breaking the rules and that only the young know which new rules to break. It can be a person with an I'm-not-from-here accent who is viewed as not having the "leadership skills" to manage a group. It can be anyone—white, African American, Latino, Asian, Indian, native American, male, female, skinny, overweight, young, or old—who encounters a bias (often an unconscious bias) that puts them in a box, limiting their ability to grow.

Most of us have untapped talents that are tied to something unique in our makeup. Race, gender, physical factors, socioeconomic factors—anything that shapes us—all work together to define the talents that we either tap or fail to tap. No one taps all of his or her talents, but some talents are more easily recognized and cultivated in traditional workplaces than others.

In organizations, untapped talent becomes invisible and unrecognized or undervalued and minimized. It might be that they aren't using their skills in communication, technology, strategy, sales, or some other functional aspect of work. It might be that they are in a position that's too small for them. It might be, conversely, that they haven't been adequately developed for the position they're in. Or they may not have a mental framework to execute their talents.

The untapped mostly come from backgrounds that uniquely equip them with experiences that foster nontraditional thinking. They develop a finely tuned sense of resourcefulness, resilience, and resolve. When they draw on these experiences in a work environment, they offer fresh, innovative perspectives on organizational challenges. They become "tapped talent," and their passions and skills not only align but are applied to opportunities. Unlike the untapped, who show up just to do a job, the tapped show up to make an impact.

Identifying and developing this talent pool allows organizations to promote from within, develop a culture that stars and emerging stars want to join, reduce turnover, win the war for talent, and experience the types of lightning strikes that ignite passion and long-term success.

I wrote this book because I believe everybody has a unique purpose. In this case, uniqueness is characterized by an act, skill, or ability that inherently brings joy to a person. It may be the hotel doorman who spends 40 years greeting guests as they arrive, the postal workers who writes notes to the people along her route, or the youth worker at a homeless shelter who smiles as bright as the sun when one of her families moves into permanent housing. It may be the plastic surgeon who restores disfigured faces, the account executive who mentors new hires, or someone like Steve Jobs, who changed the world through technology.

People want to tap into their talents and feel what it's like to give birth to that distinctive purpose. When we engage people at that level of discovery, we get a full sense of their "self"—of their self-actualization. They are operating on all cylinders—mind, body, and spirit. They're using all of their natural resources. They feel energized. Their productivity is exceptional.

I believe this book will help you find and grow the talent throughout your organization that's been undervalued and underdeveloped—the talent that's been untapped. Tapping into it will change you, your organization, and the world!

Navigating Untapped Talent

This book is organized in three sections. The first provides some foundational ideas about untapped talent and why it exists. The next section covers three specific areas where leaders can directly impact an organization by mining and refining talent. The third looks at three characteristics I've identified as essential in great leaders as it applies to untapped talent.

This isn't explicitly a how-to book, but there is a good bit of how-to woven into the pages. You'll learn how to identify and develop untapped talent, and you'll also learn how to tap more successfully into your own untapped talents. One way we'll do this is through leadership exercises that show up at the end of several chapters. Use these for your own personal improvement and share them with your team members when appropriate.

LEADERSHIP EXERCISE: SETTING YOUR PATH

Early on, I want you to have a sense of your career path—its highs and lows. This exercise will help set a context for the book and the other leadership exercises that follow. You'll learn that the more you consciously know about yourself, the more chances you'll have to make different decisions.

In this leadership exercise, you'll examine when you have been successful in your career and when your talent hasn't been tapped. Identifying your successes will emphasize the difference between those successes and the times when your talent hasn't been tapped. Also, understanding your career successes and challenges will make it easier to recognize when members of your team are performing below their talent levels.

Part One

Consider a time when your career was at a high. You were in the right position, with the right manager, and working on the right assignments. Work seemed easy, not because it was, but because you were fully engaged and you were using all of your talent, skills, and abilities.

1. Describe what was happening (e.g., name the assignment and explain why it was so right).
2. What thoughts and feelings can you remember during that time? Were you exuberant, ready to go to work each morning? Were you thinking about work as fun?
3. What moved you forward to your next assignment?
4. What did you learn about yourself and your abilities?

Part Two

Consider a time when you knew you were not in the right position, with the right manager, or working on the right assignments.

1. Briefly describe what happened.
2. How did it make you feel and what were your thoughts? What did it feel like to go to work every day?
3. What did you do about the situation?
4. What did you learn about yourself and your ability?

Part Three

1. Describe the differences between when your career was working and when you were not in the right position. Be very clear about the behaviors you exhibited, how you felt, and their impact on your success.
2. How can you use what you learned about your individual experience of untapped talent in assisting your team in being more successful?

PART I
Defining

This page intentionally left blank

CHAPTER 1

The Hidden Workforce

This page intentionally left blank

> Talented people need organizations less than organizations need talented people.
>
> —Daniel Pink, author

The CEO of a Fortune 500 securities company once shared with me the one question that most keeps him up at night: "Where am I going to find the talent to lead this corporation forward?" he said. "I just don't see it."

He's not alone. Thousands of leaders are asking themselves and their talent management executives the same question. The fact is modern leaders face two harsh realities: One, the talent that once delivered corporate success no longer is good enough to meet modern corporate goals. Two, the talent needed to deliver corporate success now and in the future is scarce.

The talent that once made organizations successful isn't necessarily obsolete. It's just insufficient.

There was a time not so long ago when people and organizations interacted in a pretty limited and straightforward manner. Life and work weren't easy, and complications often arose, but there wasn't the widespread complexity that we face today.

Technological advances have greatly increased the "touch points" between organizational systems, multiplying the factors that affect every decision a person or organization makes. Trans-Atlantic conference calls at 9 PM are now the rule and not the exception for conducting business. Video conferencing, or "halo" calls, have replaced face-to-face meetings.

Text messaging is the expedient way to get in touch with someone, and the telephone is convenient but often not necessary unless things are too complicated to explain on paper.

The world—the people, the systems, the organizations—exists in increasingly interconnected ways, and interconnected systems are, by definition, more complex.

The new norm in our complex world is about differences—on multiple dimensions. Each "difference" that's introduced into a situation makes that situation more complex. It becomes a new factor that can contribute to the richness and success of the situation, but it can also present new hurdles and challenges. Such differences take a variety of forms—people, experiences, skills, worldviews, talents, relationships, politics, gender, race, social status, education, reputation... the list goes on.

Nowadays very few organizations are localized or even regionalized: they're global. Markets are expanding to the farthest reaches of the planet. More and more Americans are seeking employment in the emerging markets of Brazil, Russia, India, and China—better known as the BRIC countries—unsaturated markets that were growing at a rate of nearly three times that of developed markets[1] prior to the global economic crisis of 2008–2009 and continues today. The growth might have slowed, but these markets still provide opportunities for employment and development while building a person's global resume.

Many US corporations are building their wealth outside the country where emerging markets provide a greater return on investment. GE, United Technologies, Hasbro Inc., and MacDonald's Corp are some of the many companies that have been increasing revenues significantly overseas while their revenues in the United States have been decreasing or growing very little. GE, for instance, saw its US revenues drop 3.4 percent in the second quarter of 2011 but jump 23 percent in its international business.[2]

Also, international companies increasingly are buying US corporations and filling top leadership jobs with expatriates from other countries. In Massachusetts alone, Manulife Financial, a Canadian company, acquired John Hancock Financial; German-based Adidas Group purchased Reebok; French-based Sanofi-Aventis purchased biotech giant Genzyme; and Santander, the Spanish financial giant, acquired Sovereign Bank.

Business leaders now come from all over the world. In 1999, the QS Global 200 Business School Report listed only 15 MBA programs that were based outside of North America or Europe. By 2012, that number had grown to 51, including 36 in Asia-Pacific countries.

English is the business language of the world, but international teams often slip into their mother tongues when working in groups—it's expedient to do what comes naturally.

It's no wonder then that the United States is struggling to maintain its global competitive advantage.

So Americans are working all over the world, and the world is coming to America to work. But that's just part of the cultural complexity business leaders face now—continuing to build the sense of urgency. There's also the generational dynamics—the mixing of baby boomers, gen X, and gen Y with all their differing expectations, ways of working, and values around employment. Managing and working across generations has become one of the major challenges facing organizations.

Demographics also are shifting along ethnic lines. The number of Americans who identify themselves as "mixed-raced" has grown by more than 35 percent since 2000, while Hispanics are the fastest-growing and most influential demographic in our time, evident by their impact on the 2012 US presidential election. Latino votes made the difference in President Obama being reelected.

The talent that organizations develop and hire in the middle of these realities can't be homogeneous. But it's counterproductive and inefficient to have an organization in which everyone looks and thinks the same. A complex, globalized economy demands diverse, complex talents. Gocke Sargut and Rita Gunther McGrath put it this way in a 2011 article for *Harvard Business Review*: "Complex systems are organic; you need to make sure your organization contains enough diverse thinkers to deal with the changes and variations that will inevitably occur."[3]

While this notion may appear simplistic, it's not. One of my large pharmaceutical clients prides itself in hiring only from the "best" schools in the world—Harvard, Stanford, Penn, London Business School, INSEAD, Hong Kong UST, the Indian Institutes of Management. They look for a certain type of candidate with specific degrees and technical experience. Limiting their candidate search to Ivy League–type schools minimizes their opportunities to employ professionals who may be just as intelligent, creative, and innovative but who developed their skills through a very different path.

The diversity of someone's path can add incredible value and perspective to their problem-solving abilities and innovative thought. Some professionals may have attended state universities for undergraduate work and then gone on to a more elite school for graduate work. Others may have found summer internships in local nonprofits, gaining experiences that add significant value to their resumes but that lacked the perceived value that comes with an internship at a Fortune 500 company. Or they might have earned their college educations later in life after years of taking night classes.

For modern organizations to achieve success, they have to find talent that looks, thinks, and acts differently from the norm. Anything less simply isn't good enough.

Scarce Talent: The Skills Gap

This dovetails into the second reality that modern leaders face: Right talent is scarce.

In 1997, a McKinsey & Company research project on talent management practices and beliefs coined the term "war for talent." They updated their findings in 2000, by which time they had surveyed roughly 13,000 managers at 112 large US companies. The surveys examined the existing and developing needs of corporate employers and compared these needs to the skills and talents of the workforce.

The reality painted by McKinsey (and subsequent research by others) hasn't changed in the last decade: The available talent required for success in US companies is shrinking and companies aren't prepared for it. Start-ups, midsize companies, and large corporations all need more than bodies to fill seats—they need sophisticated talent that understands global issues, multicultural influences, technology, and how to navigate in increasingly delayered organizational structures. This is particularly relevant in health care, business services, leisure and hospitality, construction, manufacturing, and retail—the industries that account for more than two-thirds of employment.

"The caliber of a company's talent increasingly determines success in the marketplace," the 2001 McKinsey report said. "At the same time, attracting and retaining great talent is becoming more difficult, as demand for highly skilled people outstrips supply."[4]

This doesn't mean there are or will be fewer workers. In fact, there are far more workers than available jobs, and that's not likely to change any time soon. The world population continues to grow and baby boomers, in part because of hard economic times, aren't retiring as early as once predicted.

McKinsey released research in 2011 predicting a need for 21 million jobs to bring the United States back to full employment by 2020.

So why are corporate employers struggling to fill the openings they have with qualified workers? There's a skills gap.

"Under current trends, the United States will not have enough workers with the right education and training to fill the skill profiles of the jobs likely to be created," McKinsey reported. "Our analysis suggests a shortage of up to 1.5 million workers with bachelor's degrees or higher in 2020…The configuration of the labor force will not neatly fit the requirements of employers."[5]

In some cases, Americans simply aren't learning the skills that a changing corporate world needs. There is a misalignment between the skills of the unemployed and those needed to fill many of the jobs in our technical world. Our school systems have been very slow in adapting curricula to meet the needs of today's marketplace. American schools are continuing to teach repetition and memory techniques as opposed to critical thinking, science, math, language, and basic living and leadership curriculum skills. But that's a totally different book.

While the overall talent pool is growing, some parts of it—parts that often have many of the skills relevant to the changing marketplace—are shrinking. More and more of the best talent, including those fresh out of college, are opting for a trip down the entrepreneurial highway, either starting their own businesses or leaving the corporate world for smaller companies.

Most corporate leaders take one or two approaches to these challenges. They buy proven rock stars or invest in workers who most obviously demonstrate high potential.

These tactics, however, simply aren't enough.

Buying talent is expensive and often proves detrimental to the existing corporate culture. It contributes to an organization's struggle to develop a reliable culture because it has little or no institutional memory on its payroll and because it has such a constant infusion of new ideas and people. Or it rejects new solutions to existing challenges because those solutions don't fit the norm. Leaders come and go without making an impact—the very reason they were hired.

As McKinsey's research confirms, the pool of traditional emerging talent—those with required skills who are easy for managers to spot—has shrunk. Thus, an insufficient, relatively small percentage of an organization's workforce ends up with the right assignments, the right mentors, the right coaching, and the right training for developing its potential.

Being in the "right" everything is that rare situation when your expertise, training, experience, and opportunity come together, allowing you to maximize your talent. So what employers need is to expand the pool of workers they can develop by giving them the "right" everything. Where can they find these workers? In a place I call the "hidden workforce."

Defining the Hidden Workforce

The corporations that stand to win are the ones that mine the talent that's already in the economy but going untapped—the hidden workforce. I will focus more specifically on how organizations can do this better in a later chapter, but for now let's look at what this hidden workforce is.

People in the hidden workforce typically perform at an acceptable level, get decent but not career-advancing assignments, and move from month to month and year to year in an invisible, uninspiring space. Or, they have performed above average and steadily advanced, and then find their careers in a stall and can't figure out what's needed to change their trajectories.

They lose sight of their potential. They don't know how to present that potential, nor are they motivated to present it. Their managers, meanwhile, don't recognize or acknowledge that potential. So everyone simply accepts a status quo—a misinformed dictate that limits the person's success, the manager's success, and the organization's success.

Great organizations *selectively* recruit the very unique talent they need, but they also routinely find and develop the internal talent that other organizations overlook. They don't just rely on their "A" players; they bring out something better in their "B" and "C" players—or the ones who really were "A" players all along, but just didn't realize it.

They find their Susan Boyle.

"Susie Simple," as she was nicknamed while growing up in Scotland, was diagnosed with a learning disability, and the only real job she ever had was as a trainee cook. She took some singing lessons, but mainly performed at her church or at karaoke pubs when she wasn't taking care of her aging mother. She was nearly 50 when she auditioned for *Britain's Got Talent*, the British version of *American Idol*. She was overweight, made no attempts to glamorize her plain appearance, and came across as socially awkward.

She was rather coldly received by the audience and judges when she first walked on stage. Few seemed to take her seriously as a performer.

I'd suggest that you watch the YouTube video for yourself, but with more than 80 million "views," chances are you've already seen it at least once.

After her brief onstage interview with the judges, Boyle, in a powerful mezzo-soprano voice, brought the crowd to its feet with her rendition of "I Dreamed a Dream" from *Les Misérables*. She eventually finished in second place on the television show, but the one-time Catholic choir girl became an international star.

"Modern society is too quick to judge people on their appearances," she later told *The Washington Post*. "There is not much you can do about it; it is the way they think; it is the way they are. But maybe this could teach them a lesson, or set an example." Susie demonstrated perfectly the power of untapped talent.

Hiding in Plain Sight

Susan Boyle isn't the exception. She's not just a rare and hidden gem, not just a needle in a hundred fields of haystacks. She's simply a well-known example of someone who emerged from the hidden workforce once others recognized and appreciated her previously untapped talents.

But perhaps you can relate better to a friend of mine that I'll call "Jill Rogers."

Jill is a 42-year-old mother of two children. She manages the learning and development department for a $5 billion organization with 30,000 employees worldwide. Her career has progressed steadily over the years from manager to senior manager to director and now senior director. Jill is vivacious, enjoys people, is a stellar performer and a valued colleague. She's the type of person that everyone likes to work with and for.

Jill and I were together a few years ago during an executive leadership retreat, and I saw a woman who, frankly, didn't want to be seen and I didn't recognize. She could have stayed hidden in her room, but she did something worse—she was hiding in plain sight. She hardly spoke during the workshops at the retreat. On that rare occasion when she spoke, her voice was barely audible and her words were delivered without conviction, although there was clear thinking behind them. She spent much of the time looking down at the table with her face hidden by her hair. Jill had become a shadow of the woman I'd first met a few years earlier—bright, energetic, and courteous in thought and action. I couldn't help but wonder: What happened?

As the retreat went on, I had the opportunity to sit with her over coffee to ask a few pointed questions.

"I don't know what's happened to me," she said.

I feel like I've lost a part of who I am. My confidence isn't there. People don't pay attention to what I'm saying. I even sound different to me. Every time I turn in a project to my manager, it comes back with red lines all over it and long paragraphs in the margins. Her comments are helpful, but I'm never certain what she wants or what she's looking for because the written instructions are always different than what we discussed. It seems she and everyone else ignores me during staff meetings, and my contact with senior leaders is being monitored closely. Worst of all, I'm corrected constantly in front of my peers and staff. This isn't going to end well.

Jill felt marginalized in her job and, as a result, was showing signs of insecurity and a lack of confidence. She had lost her voice. She had slipped, unintentionally, into the hidden workforce and many of her talents remained untapped.

My advice (short version): Pull your hair back, show your face, and go speak the truth. Your voice has power. You're smart, clever, and resourceful. Take charge of your career.

I'd like to report that Jill got the message in one take, but, of course, we had several rounds of coaching conversations over a couple of months. Eventually, Jill did take charge. She took responsibility for herself and stopped letting her circumstances define her. She transferred to a different division within her company where her skills were being used to their full capacity, and she's once again thriving—a radiant, confident, passionate contributor to her organization's success. The transformation was amazing. She's shinning from the inside out. By the way, as I write this chapter, Jill is in line for a major promotion to vice president.

We'll talk more in later chapters about how the Jill Rogers and Susan Boyles of the world can make such a transformation—what they can do and how managers and other leaders can help make that happen. For now, the point is that they aren't alone. They found their way out of the hidden workforce, but they also represent the millions of people who, for one reason or another, aren't fully tapping into the talents that reside within them.

Some percentage of what people in the hidden workforce have to offer—and that percentage differs for everyone—goes untapped. Ironically, the people who fall short of their potential often appear as if they have achieved the upper-middle-class American dream. Some are obviously underemployed, but most are more like Jill. Their careers as middle- and senior-level leaders provide a comfortable living. Family and community nod to their successes. But they never experience that place of total gratification around their careers. Internally, they lack peace; they feel a lingering hunger from dreams unfulfilled, a desire that slowly turns into frustration and then, for some, a lack of engagement. As untapped talent, they show up each day to do a job. They live out the slogan "The dead come alive at five." *I did my part today*, they think, *now let's get on with life*.

They aren't just hidden. They are, in a word, unhappy.

The Pursuit of Happiness

Most of us aren't unhappy all the time, but most of us are unhappy some of the time. That's life, right? We ride the ebbs and flows like rafters on the Colorado River, gently floating along during some stretches and holding on for dear life when we crash down the rapids.

When you find yourself in the hidden workforce, you likely find that you aren't fully engaged in your work, and that affects your productivity and your happiness. You know something's missing, and something inside you says that life would be better if only you could somehow fill that void. When you can't pinpoint it or address it, you disengage or engage less.

When that happens, you lose. When that happens with the people on your team, your team and you lose. And your organization loses. And your customers and clients lose. And your community loses.

You get the idea. Nobody wins.

Jennifer Robison, reporting in *Gallup Management Journal* on a study on employee engagement released in 2010, pointed out that there's "a clear link between engagement and profitability, which makes engagement a more urgent issue."[6] And most organizations recognize the importance of employee engagement. Julia Kirby, who wrote "The Economics of Well-Being" for the *Harvard Business Review*, told the *Chicago Tribune* that she doesn't know of "any major company that doesn't do employee satisfaction surveys or measures of employee engagement."[7]

Unfortunately, research by Gallup, which has tracked employee engagement for more than a decade, continues to indicate organizations aren't having much impact on developing a more engaged workforce.

In 2010, Gallup's surveys showed that 54 percent of American workers were "not engaged," meaning they had "essentially 'checked out.' They're sleep walking through their workday, putting time—but not energy or passion—into their work." Another 18 percent were "actively disengaged," meaning they acted out their unhappiness in ways that undermined others. That left only 28 percent as "engaged" in their work—working with passion and driving their organizations forward with innovation.

Year-by-year comparisons show very little change in these statistics.

So here's the sad reality: While most of us go through phases of disengagement in our work, millions are stuck in the hidden workforce. They are chronically disengaged. They actually "shrink" the workforce simply by living and working below their potential. Add up the lost productivity of all these underperformers—10 percent for Jack in accounting, 5 percent for Marlene in marketing, multiplied times the millions who fit in this category—and we see a substantial hidden workforce that undoubtedly cost the economy billions of dollars each year. Indeed, Gallup calculates that actively disengaged employees—the least productive—cost the American economy up to $300 billion per year in lost productivity.[8]

You might make the argument that creating a happy workforce is the key to improving employee engagement and, therefore, increased productivity and profits. And the way to make workers happy is to give them perks. Make sure they have free parking, good food in the cafeteria, a foosball table, and free dry cleaning,...Oh, yeah, and pay them well. And don't forget to let them work from home or the coffee shop or the park.

I'm not knocking those things. They have a place, but they can take on many different forms and be ineffective in their approach to increase productivity and engagement. The foosball table might help build an engaged culture in one organization and have no impact, or even a negative impact, in another culture. A small organization might not have a cafeteria, much less good food to put in it. Free parking might not matter if most of the workers bike or walk to work. And research shows that pay incentives work to increase functional, task-focused skills but they don't promote creativity or employee engagement.[9]

The point is that there is no one-size-fits-all list of benefits for building a happy workforce. People don't leave organizations, they leave managers. Many are searching for acknowledgment of a job well done, guidance, and direction as means to pull them into full engagement. Most don't receive the fine art of "good management."

Not only that but "happy" isn't always everything it's cracked up to be. June Gruber, an assistant professor of psychology at Yale, told the *Boston Globe* in a 2011 article that social scientist have "put happiness under the microscope just like we do with every other mental state, and we see that there is this dark side."[10]

The preponderance of research shows that happiness correlates to better physical and mental health, flexible thinking, creativity, and better social skills. But researchers like Gruber point out that happy people also can miss the warning signs that sad people spot because they're scanning for trouble. And, ironically, people who emphasize the pursuit of happiness tend to be more self-absorbed, resulting in loneliness and disappointment. Indeed, research[11] indicates that people who are *truly* consistently happy aren't those who chase after it; instead, the consistently happy ones are those with a healthy self-awareness and a commitment to serving others and the greater good.

That's why the most important benefits an organization can offer its employees is work that taps into their talents. And, to make it personal, the most important thing we can pursue in our work isn't "happiness" but to put into practice the talents we've been given.

For organizational leaders that involves creating and painting a vision you really believe in and that others can buy into. But it can't stop there. For example, I can believe in the vision of thousands of organizations—this one wants to cure cancer, this one wants to put shoes on the feet of the shoeless in Africa, this one wants to develop the next big Internet innovation. Lots of causes are worthy; lots of businesses have big and wonderful ideas and ideals. But where do I fit in that vision? As a leader, you have to help me answer that question. We have to figure out where and how my untapped talents will drive the vision that's so grand. Then I can really engage in my work—and your vision.

I like the way the late theologian Howard Thurman summed up this concept: "Don't ask yourself what the world needs; ask yourself what makes you come alive. And then go and do that. Because what the world needs is people who have come alive."

When we tap into our talents, we come alive. When we come alive, we're passionate and engaged in our work. When we're passionate and engaged in our work, we're productive and happy. Then we can emerge from the hidden workforce and make the most of life.

LEADERSHIP EXERCISE: ASSESSING YOUR HIDDEN WORKFORCE

Now that you understand the dynamics of the hidden workforce, it's time to assess whether any of your team members are potential candidates or current members of the hidden workforce. This is a short but revealing assessment that can guide your team to better results:

- Briefly state your organization's business goals for the year.
- What are your team's business goals, and how do they track to the overall goals of the business?
- Review the performance plans and progress to date of your team members and their direct reports. Track the ratings and progress against goals for each member of your team.
- Based on the performance ratings, track the top one-third, the middle one-third, and the bottom one-third. Compare you team's engagement scores with your assessment of their performance.
- What patterns emerge? Is everyone's progress moving the team forward? Are there any surprises? If so, what are they?
- Who are the members of your team who may be in the hidden workforce? What lead you to make this determination?
- What options are available for you as a leader to improve the team's performance? Is there an opportunity to coach and develop those who need to improve their performances? Who must you engage to assist with improving the efficiency and productivity of your team?

CHAPTER 2

Why Talent Goes Untapped

This page intentionally left blank

People are overlooked for a variety of biased reasons and perceived flaws: Age, appearance, personality.

I believe that there is a championship team of twenty-five people that we can afford, because everyone else in baseball undervalues them.

—Peter Brand, in the movie *Moneyball*

You've no doubt read or heard about the famous "win-win" outcomes of life. Maybe you've even experienced a few of them. You make a deal or otherwise reach an agreement with someone and, when it's done, you and the other person both win.

Pop the cork on the champagne. Strike up the band. Let the party begin. Or, at the very least, walk away with a smile, feeling good about life.

When people (or organizations) can align on common goals, they can partner and work toward a win-win outcome. It happens all the time—five of the six major airlines, for instance, partnered to create Orbitz. But, of course, it doesn't happen often enough. Sometimes people or organizations *can't* work together toward a common goal because they have competing interests. Competing ad agencies might partner on a campaign to promote a charity event, but one agency must lose when they go head-to-head for a major client. Other times, however, people or organizations *won't* work together toward a common goal; they lack the know-how, the desire, the vision, the commitment, and so on.

It's easy to accept the competitive realities of life—the unavoidable rivalries between baseball teams or businesses. What's frustrating is when everyone agrees on the goals, but they can't seem to pull together to create obviously desirable outcomes. For instance, none of us see untapped talent as a *good* thing, either for individuals or for the organizations that employ them. Rightly, we all want to live up to our potential. We all want to come alive in our work. We all want the satisfaction of a life well lived. And organizations want happy, efficient workers who are contributing in every way possible.

So why is it so hard to achieve this particular win-win? Why does so much talent go untapped?

Discovering the Realities

Through 30 years of consulting work and after conducting hundreds of organizational climate assessments on inclusion, diversity, leadership, team effectiveness, and performance with mid- and large-size corporations in a cross-section of industries, I've identified what I call "inhibitor environments." These are the environments that leave talent devalued and thus untapped.

Some fundamental realities of human nature shape these inhibitor environments. And a basic understanding of these realities can help us reshape the outcomes—it can help us move toward a win-win in which talent no longer goes untapped. The best way to understand these inhibitor environments is with a common understanding of what untapped talent looks like and how it manifests within these environments. Here's when it happens.

Talent Is Devalued and Therefore Untapped When a Person Lacks Access

Access is one of the greatest nontangible levers to success. A single act of connecting with the right person who can provide you with the right information has changed many careers. When I work with clients, here's how I define access: "Providing entry to an influential person(s) or being placed in a career situation that broadens your perspective and skill base." Access raises the curtains to the rooms that are invisible to many but well-known by a select few—the power brokers in an organization.

One global leadership assessment conducted by a $35 billion corporation revealed that access, opportunity, and development were the major factors that could increase the representation of women at its senior levels.[1]

Like most global corporations, this organization did well when it came to hiring and developing female professionals below the vice president level. Breaking through that wall where one became an officer of the company, however, was a very different story. Women represented 42 percent of the organization's workforce, but only 25 percent of its leaders who were a vice president or higher.

Through the extensive research described earlier and discussions with women in Europe, Asia, Latin America, and the United States, this corporation discovered advancement requires a certain amount of exposure to leaders other than one's manager. Observing senior leaders in action—working with them on taskforces or on corporatewide assignments—helps aspiring talent understand the behaviors, mindsets, and temperaments required for senior leadership. Exposing developing talent to the operating models of leadership provides a well-defined roadmap to success. Without building relationships with upper-level leaders, it's almost impossible to advance in the competitive corporate environment. They need clout-wielding advocates to speak up for them and raise their names as potential candidates for strategic assignments.

In other words, they need sponsorship, a strategy that is proving more effective than mentoring. Sponsors have organizational influence and access to the inner circles of the organization. They can broaden the visibility of a person's talents across senior leadership, creating networking opportunities and advocates for a person's next career move.

In the past, sponsorships were based mainly on informal working relationships. There weren't many structured programs. Leaders created teams based on the people they valued and trusted, but they primarily valued and trusted what was familiar and comfortable. They didn't intentionally invest in or surround themselves with people who weren't naturally on their radar, thus perpetuating the "good old boy" network that's a hallmark of an inhibitor environment. While this tribalism still exists (and we'll get into the "why" in subsequent chapters), we're seeing more and more formal sponsorships that help break the glass ceilings that exist for women, people of color, veterans, baby boomers, and others who are not considered in the mainstream.

Access isn't just about sponsors; equally important are the resources that support success. I've coached a number of newly appointed leaders through their 90-day transition plans. When we explore their resources to "accomplish the job," additional staff and budgets are almost always lacking, especially in a tight economy that puts a premium on doing more with less.

Yes, being resourceful and making the most of your relationships inside your work environment is critical, but that doesn't make up for the additional set of hands or expertise that's needed to accomplish a goal. Short budgets can translate into less effective outcomes. Less effective outcomes diminish the corporation, the manager and leader's success—it's a lose-lose.

The final key element of access is ongoing, constructive, and critical feedback. The development and enrichment of skills and the ability to build confidence in professionals is predicated on sitting down more than once a year and sharing your perceptions with the people you're trying to develop. Great managers make this a part of their daily lives and weekly interactions. They constantly guide and instruct and coach their people to success. Quick five-minute coaching conversations on approaches to people and situations can minimize stress, ward off setbacks, and build long-term success. Sharing this information with rising talent also requires that leaders have keen observation skills.

What I often observe and hear from leaders are comments such as "my manager seldom responds to my emails and only provides feedback after the fact." Or "my manager only provides feedback at performance review time" (a little late to make midyear corrections). Or "my manager just isn't that interested, unless you're being put on a performance action plan. That generally means that in two months you're on your way out the door." I frequently ask managers, "If you don't communicate what's expected—what success is—and guide someone through the process, how can you expect positive results?" They seldom have a response to the question but it's clear the wheels are turning in their heads.

Everyone, no matter how senior or outstanding their work, needs feedback. It may vary in frequency, scope, and importance as you become more and more mature in your professional role, but it's still needed. Unfortunately, we cannot always see ourselves as we truly are; we must depend on the insights of others to reinforce, redirect, and affirm our behaviors.

Talent Is Devalued and Therefore Untapped When a Lack of "Fit" Exists between the Talent, the Work, and the Organization

Most organizations want people who "fit in" and who "stand out." In other words, they want people who fit the culture and who excel in their work. In some organizations, in fact, cultural fit is more important than skill, because there's a belief that skills often are more easily taught than the elusive "cultural fit."

Indeed, hiring people who "fit"—who easily work within the established norms and nuances of the culture, and who share the same vision and values—is important to organizational success. And individuals should seek organizations where they will "fit," as well.

Every organizational culture develops norms for what success means, for what leadership looks like, for what it takes to get promotions, and for the key assignments that lead to advancement. But some leaders become blinded by their mental model of cultural fit and miss out on talent they could hire or marginalize the talent that's already around them. They suffer from just-like-me myopia and lean too heavily on informal relationships within the organization. When it's time to give out a plum assignment or fill a position, they end up giving the assignment or the job to the same types of people over and over again. They eventually develop mental models that limit their choices, thus devaluing the other talent around them and leaving it untapped.

If a person's talents don't fit the organizational norms, that person's true talents can become hard to spot or appreciate, much less develop. In a documentary I helped developed for a large, multinational company, one of the employees explained this phenomenon: "[We] invest a lot of time and money recruiting very strong talent to the organization. But once we have the talent in, we tend to [indoctrinate] them to our way of thinking, our practices, and our approaches. We don't necessarily have an openness toward new ideas that perhaps are different than the ones we're accustomed to."

Yet, there are the exceptions to the rules, the "outliers" who somehow have achieved that supreme status of being different and effective in an organization. Outliers have learned to draw attention to their unique skill, which places the value on performance and not fit. What's extraordinary in outliers' circumstances is that everyone accepts their differences. They are the odd ones out—the person on the team who has learned his/her value, can effectively display it, and engage colleagues in the pursuit of success. They are accepted as the unique ones with rare talent or depth of knowledge. Others admire them and seek them for input and help.

During my early years of consulting, I remember a case at a research lab in Denver, Colorado, where the head scientist actually walked around backward. When I first saw him, I thought, "That's a bit odd." Then someone told me, "Oh, that's Harry. He's like that and no one bothers him." Harry was different in all description but he had skills that exceeded the abilities of others—he was a scientific genius—and that alone was sufficient explanation for Harry's behavior. People simply accepted that Harry was Harry. No one cared that he walked backward, because he moved the work forward.

Talent Is Devalued and Therefore Untapped When We Fail to See That a Person's Skills May Have Multiple Uses

Vonetta Flowers dreamed of winning a gold medal in the Olympics, and that dream came true—but not until she embraced a totally different venue for her talents.

Vonetta qualified for the 1996 US Olympic Trials in the 100-meter dash and in the long jump, but she didn't make the US team. She qualified for the 2000 US Olympic Trials in the long jump, but again failed to make the team. So Flowers decided to retire from athletics and start a family.

Johnny Flowers, Vonetta's husband and also a track athlete, found himself in a similar situation, but he wasn't ready to give up on his Olympic dreams. So he responded to a flyer he read that was looking for athletes—men and women—who might be willing to trade in their track spikes for ice spikes. Instead of asking for athletes who wanted to run and jump in the warm sun, the flyer sought people willing to push a 450-pound bobsled, jump aboard, and steer it down a narrow icy track at speeds of up to 80 miles an hour.

Johnny asked his wife to join him in trying out for the US bobsled team, but Vonetta wasn't interested. She went with him for his tryout, however, and when he injured his hamstring and had to drop out of the trials, Vonetta finally agreed to give the women's team a shot. She qualified, made the team, and, on February 19, 2002, the 28-year-old from Birmingham, Alabama, partnered with Jill Bakken to win a gold medal at the Winter Olympics in Park City, Utah.

"My goal was to make the Summer Olympics," she told the Associated Press after the winning the race. "God had a different plan for me."

Vonetta became the first African American to win a gold medal at the Winter Olympics, and it started when someone posted a flyer at the US Olympic Trials. That person—and I'd love to send him or her a thank-you note—suspected that talented athletes who traditionally competed in the summer heat could excel in the snow and ice of a winter sport. That person knew people like Vonetta had talents that simply needed to be planted in a different field. Then they could bloom, even in the cold of winter.

Inhibitor environments don't recognize that talent is transferrable—that it can be reshaped and reformed and thrive in totally different contexts. When we pigeonhole people into jobs and situations, we prevent them from finding new outlets for their existing talents and discovering new talents they didn't even know existed.

Consider Liz Walker, the Emmy-winning news anchor who left journalism to become a minister and to run a public relations firm. Or Ruth Ellen Fitch, the lawyer who is now CEO of The Dimock Center, a major health-care center. Both will tell you that their new situations required new ways of thinking and working and that the early phases were extremely challenging but not without reward. Both will tell you that the change brought something new and different in their lives that they hadn't expected: They were living more fully because they were using different skills and abilities. Their old jobs seemed like two lifetimes ago. Yet, if not for those early trainings and experiences, they know they wouldn't have been ready for their new assignments in life.

Talent Is Devalued and Therefore Untapped When a Person Isn't Ready and/or Prepared for an Opportunity (or Vice Versa)

Some people advance their careers without the necessary preparation for handling their new assignments. They didn't get the necessary stretch assignments along the way. They missed out on the step-by-step-by-step process of professional development that most corporations employ. They didn't receive adequate performance-related feedback. They didn't learn how to best use their skills or develop their talents through proper training and mentoring. Most important, they didn't have a sponsor who would elevate their presence and speak up for their performance. So they ended up marginalized in their new role.

Sometimes they were promoted into jobs they didn't really aspire to or want, but they felt like they couldn't turn down the offer. For instance, they took a job that required significant operational skills (which they lacked) and little conceptual thinking skills (which they possessed). They ended up needing guidance and mentoring to succeed with the job, which may have made them appear less competent and which led to fewer new assignments.

Conversely, people sometimes take new positions assuming they understand what their new leader needs and wants based on the interview discussions and posthiring meetings. An alluring picture has been painted of the job. Then they discover that the standards and operating norms of a department and, more importantly, a leader didn't align with the job description.

For instance, one woman I've worked with took a high-level job leading an international products development team. Her supervisors indicated they wanted her in the job partly because of her take-charge, straightforward approach and her big-picture perspective. In reality, they were accustomed to running their own show—setting a vision for others to execute, not debate.

"It was a Catch-22," she told me.

> From a product development standpoint, I always pushed strategy. I pushed for more than what leaders have become accustomed to. I think they wanted someone tactical—someone who would take orders, not talk a lot, and just deliver. They said they wanted someone who was creative and dynamic who could do strategy. But they weren't really ready for someone who actually did that.

Sometimes we find ourselves in the tenuous situation of having accepted a position that was too small for our skills and leadership level. As this friend discovered, it sometimes appears the job is too big for the person who took it or that the person was ill-prepared to take the helm when, in reality, the job wasn't ready for the person.

Talent Is Devalued and Therefore Untapped When a Person Doesn't Resemble the People Who Traditionally Have Held Mainstream Positions

I spent some time working with the CIA at its headquarters outside of Washington DC, and one day while having lunch in the cafeteria I noticed a group of eight or ten people sitting together and carrying on a conversation in sign language. When I thought of the typical CIA employee, nondescriptive, intelligent, hard-working, and loyal were adjectives that came to mind. "Deaf" wasn't a descriptor that I would have used. But it occurred to me that day that the ability to read lips might come in handy if you work in the intelligence industry!

We typecast people all the time, don't we? We go to the store and ask a clerk in one of the aisles for help locating a product, only to learn she isn't a clerk but a customer who is dressed the way we envision a clerk would dress.

We do the same thing in corporate settings. Sometimes our filters are so strong that we typecast people based on the most basic of characteristics. We're in a vendor meeting, for instance, and a salesperson continues to direct all her attention to the male at the head of the table. What the salesperson learns later is the leader of the team was the woman sitting in the middle seat on the other side of the table.

In America, for instance, we have a prototype of a CEO. He's six feet tall and white. How do I know this? For starters, a few years ago I saw the pictures of the top 100 CEOs in a national magazine. It struck me that I felt I was looking at the same man from picture to picture. Very few differences separated them in look. In *Blink*, Malcom Gladwell describes a survey he did of about half of the companies on the Fortune 500 list. He found, of course, that most of the CEOs were white men, but he also learned that most of those CEOs were tall, averaging just under six feet tall. That's about three inches taller than the average American male (who is five feet, nine inches tall). Almost a third of the corporations he surveyed had a CEO who was six-two or taller, compared with 3.9 percent of the adult male population in the United States.[2]

Only 18 Fortune 500 companies, meanwhile, had a female CEO in 2011 and only 3.2 percent of publically traded companies had a female CEO (98 female CEOs in 3,049 publically traded companies).[3] And as of April 1, 2011, there had only been 11 black chairmen or CEOs of Fortune 500 companies—ever.[4]

Physical appearance plays a major role in how we evaluate people. Research demonstrates that attractive people are hired more frequently than their unattractive counterparts. For women, physical attractiveness typically plays an even larger role than for men, sometimes in a negative way and sometimes in a positive one. One study, for instance, looked at whether physical attractiveness was an advantage on things like performance evaluations. It found, among other things, that it's an advantage for women in nonmanagerial positions, a disadvantage for women in managerial roles, and had no effects on reactions to men.[5]

As we build mental models on how we think people "should" look, we connect their appearances to professions. We have mental images of what people should look like if they are a janitor, an accountant, a professor, a manager, a graphic designer, a CEO, or a singer (remember the Susan Boyle story?). And once we have the mold firmly integrated into our filter system, that's often where it remains.

What's the mold made of? Half-truths and assumptions generated by our filter system—a system created from our life experiences and one that includes factors such as education, where we grew up, religious beliefs, culture, economic status, race, gender, age, sexual orientation, whether we are parents, or veterans, and so on. All of these factors inform our worldview and our worldview helps create our modes of thinking about who should be in a certain position.

Consider the qualifications for president of the United States. The Constitution says you have to be a natural born citizen and you have to be at least 35 years old. Voters, it seems, also prefer if you're male and at least six feet tall. James Madison, at five feet, four inches, was the shortest president of the United States, but 18 US presidents were (or are) at least six feet tall, and America hasn't had a top leader shorter than five feet, ten-and-a-half inches since Jimmy Carter (five feet, nine-and-a-half inches).

In our media-driven age, presidential candidates know they have to look the part—they have to look "presidential." President Obama (six feet, one inch tall, in case you're wondering) may have been acutely aware that if people couldn't imagine him as the president of the United States, he would never become the first African American to hold that position. During his campaign, he slowly began to appear "more presidential"—more stately, more conversant on the issues, more visionary, more commanding, and so forth. International trips were orchestrated to fix voters' minds on his ability to be taken seriously by global leaders. He did everything possible to communicate, "I'm like you. I know you and I will do right by you." America stepped forward and changed history in the 2008 election. We ridded ourselves of the ingrained belief that a black person could not be elected to the highest office in the land, and by reelecting

President Obama in 2012 reinforced the notion that success at the highest level in America can be obtained by anyone.

When an organization can't see past the traditional view of what certain people should look like in certain jobs, it inhibits some of its best talent from developing. The guy with tattoos, the woman from an economically deprived background who needs help learning to dress professionally, the man who always wears a starched white shirt and a tie—they all can have talents that will go untapped if those around them limit them to a stereotype.

Talent Is Devalued and Therefore Untapped When Inclusion Is Not a Leadership Practice in an Organization

Inclusion happens when every colleague feels valued, engaged, supported, and respected. This is easier said than done, but it can be accomplished.

Eastman Gelatine, a small manufacturing plant in Peabody, Massachusetts, demonstrated the power that full participation and seeking the opinions of others could have in a turnaround situation. Tasked by its corporate office, Kodak, with moving its operating numbers from a negative to a positive return on assets (ROA), Eastman Gelatine launched an organization reinvention strategy that involved the entire plant, from president to machine operators. For the first time, business plans were explained and shared with all employees and all employees had a say in how best to perform their tasks.

In less than 18 months, the numbers on the ledger began moving north. Employees, some with English as a second language, began working longer hours and charted higher levels of productivity. Communication improved up, down, and across the organization. The company also reported more cohesive team dynamics.

What was the secret? Each leader at every level began seeking people to gain their perspectives. Community and team meetings were held that asked for inputs from unusual suspects on vital topics of operation. Ideas were being put into action that previously had only been discussed in the cafeteria on breaks. Leaders began modeling a style of management that proved everyone's voice and ideas mattered. Employees were given the opportunity to learn the new skills required to operate the plant. While some struggled with English, they excelled at some of the math requirements to be successful. A fractured organization came together—everyone felt included, engaged, supported, and respected.

Eastman Gelatine taped into the value of diversity of thought, perspective, skills, and experience. On the other hand, when people feel like they don't have a voice at the table—that their ideas are ignored and dismissed—they slowly begin to disappear right in plain sight and many leave their organizations and take their talents to competitors.

Talent Is Devalued and Therefore Untapped When It Is Devalued and Untapped

If that sounds redundant it's because it involves redundancy. When talent goes devalued and untapped, a vicious cycle takes shape that's extremely difficult to spot or break.

An organization doesn't change if its leaders get comfortable with the easy way of doing things. We all like the reliability of knowing what we're going to get, even if what we're getting isn't as good as what we might get by taking a less familiar path. We become like an eagle that walks to the edge of the cliff and, seeing only the risks, never takes the leap that allows it to soar. What's worse, we keep those around us from soaring as well. Before long, the entire organization is grounded.

The cycle leads to frustration and, at times, depression for the people within the organization.

Some lose faith in the talents they know they possess. If the world around them doesn't see those talents or appreciate them, then they reason that those talents must not be very valuable. So they stop trying to cultivate them. That's makes it all the more unlikely that others will see the talent that's untapped.

Or maybe they still value the talents they know reside within themselves, but they simply give up on advancing those talents. After hitting roadblock after roadblock after roadblock, they grow weary of the fight and slowly find themselves accepting the status quo. And everyone around them embraces that status quo, as well. This is when employees with untapped talent quit and leave—or worse, they quit and stay.

Untapped talent begets untapped talent. And so it goes.

LEADERSHIP EXERCISE: AN UNTAPPED QUIZ

Understanding why talent goes untapped is critical to building teams that are operating at maximum capacity. As a leader, once you understand some of the common inhibitors in your organization's environment, you can proactively manage the challenges that surround them. Here is a short multiple choice quiz based on the content in this chapter. In this one case, there are right and wrong answers. After you complete the quiz, check your answers against the answer key. If you got an answer wrong, go back and reread the section the question pertains to. You'll quickly grasp the concepts and move on.

1. An inhibitor environment is one that:
   A. Diminishes people's natural assertiveness.
   B. Makes it less likely that people's skills and abilities will be recognized.
   C. Discourages people from expressing their true feelings.
   D. Requires people to dress according to formal business or professional standards.

2. In the context of untapped talent, lack of access includes all of the following, *except*:
   A. Having the sponsorship of an influential leader.
   B. Being given the resources needed to do one's job effectively.
   C. Getting both constructive and critical feedback.
   D. Having the same perks and privileges as others at one's organizational level.

3. A person's talent is most likely to be untapped if he/she:
   A. Does not fit into the organization's culture.
   B. Fits so well into the organization's culture that he/she does not stand out from others.
   C. Has a skill that is so strong that it sets the person apart from his/her peers.

4. An "outlier"—someone who is different from others in the organization but possesses a unique and valued skill—is likely to be:
   A. Rejected by others in the organization.
   B. Accepted by others in the organization.
   C. Accepted only by open-minded people in the organization.

5. In an inhibitor environment, people are likely to be given assignments that require them to:
   A. Use their skills in situations very similar to ones they have experienced in the past.
   B. Quickly develop new skills to work effectively in new kinds of situations that they are ready for.
   C. Develop new skills at a slow but steady pace.

6. Talent is likely to be devalued and untapped for all of the following reasons, *except*:
   A. The person doesn't look like others who have held the position.
   B. The organization does *not* try to include everyone when seeking ideas.
   C. The person isn't prepared for a new opportunity.
   D. The person's skill set is similar to that of many other persons in the organization.

Answer key: 1. B; 2. D; 3. A; 4. B; 5. A; 6. D.

CHAPTER 3

Blame the Brain

This page intentionally left blank

> If we worked on the assumption that what is accepted as true really is true, then there would be little hope for advance.
> —Orville Wright, inventor

A significant underlying reality of human nature plays a role in why so much talent goes untapped. It seems that while our conscious mind sees the value of getting the most out of the talent in ourselves and in those around us, our unconscious bias often unwittingly conspires against it.

What do I mean by *unconscious bias*?

Simply put, we're wired to see ourselves and the world around us in biased, prejudicial ways. That reality isn't all bad. It actually saves us time on the mundane tasks of life and literally can save our lives in a threatening situation. But it can also lead us into poor judgments that produce unintended consequences, including undervaluing and underdeveloping the talent within us and that around us.

If you think "not me" when it comes to bias, then consider Mahzarin Banaji. She isn't someone you'd suspect of holding any sort of prejudice or bias; so the fact that she holds them goes a long way to explaining the deeper, underlying reason why there's so much untapped talent in the world.

Banaji, the Richard Clarke Cabot Professor of Social Ethics at Harvard University's Department of Psychology, studies bias for a living. In fact, she's been on the forefront of the study of unconscious biases and implicit associations. In the early 1990s, she helped develop an Implicit Association Test (IAT) that, according to the Project Implicit website (www.implicit.harvard.edu), "measures *implicit* attitudes and beliefs that people are either unwilling or unable to report."

The computer-based test asks participants to "pair two concepts (e.g., *young* and *good*, or *elderly* and *good*)" in a rapid-fire fashion that uncovers how their unconscious minds truly associate those concepts. The IAT helps measure unconscious biases about concepts like race, ethnicity, class, gender, and age. And when Banaji took the test, it indicated she held some unconscious biases against African Americans and the elderly.

"I am neither black nor white, and I profess to hold egalitarian race beliefs," Banaji, who was born and raised in India, told the *Harvard University Gazette* in a 2003 interview. "The results suggested that I should be skeptical about my own ability to be unbiased."

The fact is that we all operate with unconscious or implicit biases and associations—those that are beyond our normal range of awareness. In other words, we have biases that are so hidden within us that we can't consciously reject them. Shankar Vedantam, author of *The Hidden Brain*, points out that the "central feature of unconscious bias is that we are not aware of it." He coined the phrase "the hidden brain" to describe "a range of influences that manipulated us without awareness."[1]

Our biases are rooted in that part of our brain that deals with the familiar. In the early days of the human adventure, people learned to challenge the unfamiliar and embrace the familiar. If you came across a plant you'd never seen, you learned to watch as someone else took a bite of it. If he survived, you'd try it, too. And what about that cute little frog that your buddy Zork decided to look at more closely? Turned out it was a poison dart frog, so you made a mental note that these colorful creatures weren't your friend.

Self-preservation, in other words, demanded that people develop biases for and against things. And the more frequently you experienced the plant you ate or the frog that poisoned your friend, the less time you had to spend thinking about whether they were good or bad. In fact, you began transferring some of those associations to similar situations. Not only did you approach poison dart frogs with caution, but all frogs became suspicious.

Over the centuries, the human brain developed more and more shortcuts for recognizing the familiar. Our ancestors passed some of these shortcuts along to us, and others we developed through our own experiences. The unconscious brain uses these mental shortcuts—known as heuristics—to process information quickly and speed up our decision-making process. When we experience something frequently, our brain works with greater speed to process it the next time we encounter it or something very similar. Certain things, like how to tie our shoes or a healthy fear of poisonous frogs, become instinctive and part of our unconscious thinking. We don't spend time contemplating such things; they just *are.*

If I showed you a series of photos of different types of flowers, you wouldn't spend much time processing them. You'd instinctively think certain things, probably positive things about the smells or the joy you associate with getting or giving flowers. You most likely have a positive, unconscious bias when it comes to flowers, but the opposite also may be true. Flowers might represent a negative experience—perhaps because your allergies flare up every time you're around flowers and this has occurred most of your life.

In his bestseller *The Tipping Point*, Malcolm Gladwell discusses how unconscious bias and implicit associations affect society. In one chapter, Gladwell talks about the "Broken Window" theory for explaining the decrease in violent crime in New York City during the mid-1990s. In a five-year period, serious crimes dropped by 50 percent and murders declined by nearly 65 percent.

Criminologist James Q. Wilson and George Kelling, who came up with the Broken Window theory, believed disorder played a huge role in an area's crime rate. Disorder takes the form of things like aggressive panhandling, graffiti, and broken windows that go unrepaired. Such disorder sends a signal that no one cares and that anything goes. So they argued that tactics like cleaning up the graffiti on subways and cracking down on "fare busters" created order, and, in doing so, had as much or more to do with the dramatic reduction in violent crimes as other notable factors—the decline in the crack cocaine trade, the aging of the population, or improvements in the city's economy.

In simple terms, information comes at us and lands somewhere on a continuum of easy (familiar, orderly) to difficult (unfamiliar, disorderly). We process it accordingly. The conscious brain is responsible for the unfamiliar and takes its time processing information like the words in a new science textbook or a complicated business proposal involving an unfamiliar industry. Thus, it has time to recognize the exceptions to the rules. The unconscious brain deals with the familiar, so it operates quickly and spends no time looking for exceptions to what it assumes to be true.

Unfortunately, what the unconscious brain assumes is true sometimes isn't so. We become a victim of our "cognitive fluency"—the measure of how easy it is to think about something. The familiar becomes easy to think about, and we associate "easy" with "true." Tests, in fact, show that something written in simple language and/or in an easy-to-read type font is deemed more factual than the same information written poorly and/or in a hard-to-read font. In "Predicting Short-Term Stock Fluctuations by Using Processing Fluency," a scholarly article written for *Proceedings of the National Academy of Sciences*, psychologists Alter Adams and Daniel Oppenheimer outline three different studies that demonstrate easy as being more profitable. They point out, for instance, that stocks with easy-to-pronounce names tend to outperform stocks with hard-to-pronounce names (especially in the short term). This easy-is-seen-as-true reality is at the heart of just about every successful advertising, marketing, or branding campaign in history, not to mention most magic tricks.

But sometimes our unconscious brain, which, again, is built for speed and quick decision-making, gets fooled by its storehouses of experiential information. It can trip over itself. It can miss the exceptions to the rules. Consider the role the unconscious brain played in the leadership style of Mark Samuels, a successful executive in the financial services industry. Mark always assumed his early childhood experiences provided a broad perspective of people and situations. Growing up traveling from one military base to another—Germany, Japan, California, and Texas—he was always the new kid on the block and secretly resented the hazing that went on. *Why can't I be accepted for me and not have to prove myself in every situation,* he frequently thought.

Mark's father retired and the family settled in Denver. For nearly ten years he lived in the same neighborhood, went to the same school, and had the same friends. He married his college sweetheart and became very successful in the private banking division of the largest bank in America. Mark was a great manager who was willing to support his people, but he expected 100 percent loyalty and output. Mark's team was growing at an accelerated rate to meet the demands of the business and within a very short time Mark had a completely new team.

Sean, one of Mark's newest members, was feeling out of touch with the team and especially with Mark. It seemed Mark was always ribbing (friendly teasing) Sean and recommending he put in extra time to meet deadlines. At first, Sean was happy to go the extra mile, redo work product, and be the butt of friendly jokes at meetings, many initiated by Mark.

After several months of continuously having to prove himself, however, Sean asked a peer, "Does this ever stop? Will I ever be accepted for my talents and for who I am?"

"Don't worry," the peer said. "That's Mark's way of assessing who you are and how you deal with ambiguity. We've all experienced it to some degree—you more than most."

When this behavior was made apparent to Mark, he had no idea where it came from or what the source was. In fact, it was hard for him to believe it was a problem. In his mind, he was helping Sean adjust.

Mark had developed a method of assessing a new team member's ability to deal with ambiguity, stress, and being the center of attention. Somewhere in Mark's unconscious brain, he assumed entry into new situations always had to be challenging. He had developed a style of managing his team members' onboarding that was similar to his own experiences from moving from military base to military base and meeting new people.

Our life experiences, and the experiences of those we spend time around, shape our unconscious biases about ourselves and about others. And these biases form complex, interrelated networks that further shape our views of people and their talents. This can shape inaccurate negative views of people—like when we unconsciously assume a young man with a ponytail isn't adept at high-level accounting practices. But it also can shape inaccurate positive views of people.

A client experienced this when she helped hire a man for a vice president–level job. "Great resume," she said of him six months after he'd been on the job. "Great background. It's just not going to work out." Why? "Besides being a nice person," she said. "I haven't been able to pinpoint anything he's good at." The man had an MBA from a prestigious management school and had worked at some great companies. But a closer look at his career revealed a history of lackluster performances. Yet, he kept getting big jobs on the basis of his resume, and he kept building his resume because of the unconscious bias associated with the degree and former assignments.

Not only do we respond based on our unconscious biases, but also (unconsciously) to the unconscious cues others send our way—their looks, their mannerisms, their subtle shifts in posture or tone of voice.

In 2011, a Fortune 500 company hired my consulting firm, Center Focus International, Inc. (CFI), to develop a set of videos to explain what unconscious bias is and how to identify it. We selected five human resource professionals to interview for a "real position" and brought in two managers from the company to conduct the interviews. All the interviews lasted 20 minutes and were filmed by Intercultural Productions, a full-service media film company in Boston.

The debrief sessions with the managers and candidates revealed the significance unconscious bias had in shaping different perceptions and outcomes from some very similar experiences. For instance, one manager, a European male named Jean-Paul, described one of the candidates as "feisty, smart," and someone he liked. The other manager, Marcia, a white American woman, described the candidate's tone of questioning as "aggressive."

When asked what was aggressive about the candidate's questions, she said,

> I'm not sure. I just shut down during the interviews. I couldn't get something out of my head. This voice kept going around in my head. To be truthful, she reminded me of my mother. And when my mother used to ask questions in that tone, it always felt as if she were questioning my judgment, not just asking me for information.

Marcia picked up on her unconscious bias in part because she respected the opinions of her coworker, which led her to question and dissect her own feelings and opinions.

"If my co-interviewer hadn't been here, we would have missed a great candidate," she said. "Jean Paul was able to help me see what I couldn't see for myself—a very capable person, a talent we would have missed if it were not for his perspective."

Many of us, had we been in Marcia's shoes, would have gone back to our offices and reported that the job candidate was not a "good fit" for the company. Few of us are mindful and conscious of the things that trigger how we view ourselves and others. Marcia was able to ascertain that the candidate triggered some old mental tapes that were unpleasant;

the introspective work she did let her know the roadblocks were related to those tapes and not the candidate's style of interviewing.

Those triggers aren't easy to spot because we seldom feel the need to slow down and question them. "Without being aware of it," Vedantam writes in *The Hidden Brain*, "we are constantly adapting to different contexts and people, modulating not just our rhythms of speech, but the very content of our ideas."[2]

For instance, Vedantam points out that experiments show our tendency to find baby features adorable, and that leads us to trust adults with "large eyes and cherubic features over adults who do not look childlike—even when the adults with childlike features are dishonest."[3]

This bias for friendly, familiar faces also helps explain other biases. The first faces we typically see are those of our parents, other family members, and their friends. If we're born in Italy, we'll quickly learn to distinguish the subtle differences in the faces of our fellow Italians. If we suddenly find ourselves in Thailand, however, we'll likely decide that most Taiwanese look very much alike.

This might not matter much if you're on vacation for two weeks in a foreign country, but it can have a huge impact on our everyday attitudes about the people we work with, the people we work for, and the people who work for us—especially in our ever-globalizing economy.

Ultimately, unconscious bias can imprison us or free us.

We can decide that such biases are inevitable and unchangeable, and we can spend our time complaining about racism and any variety of biases that keep talent hidden. Or, as John Powell and Rachel Godsil recommended in a 2011 article for *Poverty & Race*, we can act on what we know.

"Saying bias is implicit does not rob us of our moral obligation to act—just as structures that unintentionally create racialized outcomes require a social response," Powell and Godsil wrote. "Continuing to argue about 'hidden' racism will keep us locked in a polarized debate that is ultimately impossible to win."[4]

Understanding unconscious biases can help us move beyond the idea that the way to solve the world's social ills is to "fix" the "bad" people by eradicating their biases. Traditional thinking, Vedantam writes, goes something like this: "If you educated people, and provided them with accurate information, and offered them the right incentives, and threatened them with suitable punishments, and appealed to their better natures, and marked the exits clearly, the errors would vanish. Bad outcomes had to be the product of stupidity, ignorance, and bad intentions."[5]

We know that's not true, or else we already would have educated, enlightened, punished, and informed the world enough to end smoking, teen pregnancy, suicide, drug use, and all manner of crimes against society.

Understanding and reshaping our unconscious biases has to become a bigger part of the solution. To be sure, our unconscious bias—the way we see the world and the people in it—shapes our behaviors. So if we're going to tap into our hidden talents and help those around us tap into theirs, we have to make a conscious effort to understand unconscious biases and implicit associations—ours and those of others.

LEADERSHIP EXERCISE: REDUCING UNCONSCIOUS BIAS

Unconscious bias is a natural part of life and human interaction. Our early childhood imprinting and longer life experiences help create our filters, which turn into perceptions and how we see the world. While unconscious bias is a reality, we can learn to manage and sometimes repopulate the subconscious mind.

Here are steps for addressing and reducing unconscious bias:

1. Accept and assess your imperfections. Acceptance that we have unconscious bias is a significant first step. Because without the awareness of what our biases are and how they operate, it's impossible to change them. You can assess your bias levels by taking the Implicit Association Test (IAT) discussed in this chapter. There are 13 tests that provide the insight you need to better understand yourself and how you see others.
2. Challenge your assumptions. Explore whether what you believe to be true is actually true. As a leader, you have the responsibility to act on fact and not operating assumptions. Sometimes checking your assumptions is as easy as asking the difficult questions and waiting for the correct answer. If the correct answer doesn't align with your assumption, you may find yourself negotiating against your emotions. What you believe and feel may be in direct conflict with what is accurate. Make a list of your assumptions regarding a situation, decision, or person. How did your assumptions influence or impact, positively or negatively, the situation, decision, or your view of the person? What drove your assumptions? Data, experiences, and so on?
3. Seek feedback from others. Once you have explored your assumptions and how they developed and their impact, seek feedback. Collecting data from others can be challenging and difficult, especially when we are predisposed to a particular outcome. However, we must forge forward and ask the difficult questions of peers, managers, team members, and others who may not align with our judgment at times. You want as many perspectives as possible; don't stay in the realm of line-of-sight.

4. Expand the possibility of a different reality. There are always numerous stories that can make up a reality. Don't let yourself stay stuck on a "single story." Explore the new data you've collected about yourself, others, and a situation. Are you seeing things a bit different? Could you possibly open yourself up to a life with a different perspective? If yes, you are ready for the next step.
5. Discuss the "undiscussables" with the appropriate parties. When we bring a situation into the open, it helps move an issue along. During these conversations, demonstrate understanding and active listening by acknowledging the perspectives of others. List what you've learned and identify what will be different for you going forward.
6. Reinforce your behavior by holding check-ins to make sure you are staying on course.

PART II

Mining and Refining

This page intentionally left blank

CHAPTER 4

Organizational Change: Tapping the 70 Percent

This page intentionally left blank

> To exist is to change, to change is to mature, to mature is to go on creating oneself endlessly.
> —Henri L. Bergson, French philosopher and Nobel Prize winner

Jack Welch's now-famous 20–70–10 talent appraisal system provides a convenient way of grouping employees within an organization.

Welch, who led General Electric for 20 years and took it from a $13 billion company to a $500 billion megacorporation, segmented workers into three groups—the 20 percent who were the top performers, the 10 percent at the bottom, and the 70 percent who fall in between.

"You should take the top 20 percent of your employees and make them feel loved," Welch has said. "Take the middle 70 percent and tell them what they need to do to get into the top 20 percent."[1]

The bottom 10 percent? You manage them "out" of the company.

It's within that 70 percent of the workforce that you'll find the vast majority of your organization's untapped talent. Most organizations, however, develop an extremely small slice of that pie. And many leaders look into that 70 percent in search of the people who look just like them, who went to the right schools, who have the right boxes checked on their resumes. They scan the field with glasses colored by their unconscious assumptions and implicit associations.

The real talent pool—those who actually stand a chance of getting the opportunities for advancement into the top 20 percent category—shrinks to a miniscule number. You can tell everyone in that 70 percent what it takes to get into the top 20 percent, but that's not going to accomplish the job. Most of them slip into the hidden workforce; they become untapped talent. To make the most of the talent in that 70 percentile group, you have to create a culture of talent stewardship that convinces them that they really can get there, that identifies them, and that provides the path and the resources to get them there.

Without that, the best talent management systems in the world will end up tapping the same thing: The status quo.

Tapping untapped talent optimizes the performance in your organization by engaging those potential leaders who fall below that magical 20 percent threshold that most talent management programs focus on. It includes those people who execute on the day-to-day activity but may not be involved in creating the strategy. Yet, if we fail to prepare all levels of the organization for their next levels of leadership, we stumble at building an organization that can sustain itself against the mighty winds of marketplace change.

As leaders, we still want to embrace the top 20 percent of the organization, but our organizational survival depends on our ability to mine that next 70 percent in a more efficient, effective way. Since the status quo fights against such efforts, the efforts require thoughtful implementation of organized change. In the coming chapters, we'll look at three specific areas where you as a leader/manager can direct your efforts to mine and refine this untapped talent—by shaping a culture of talent stewardship, by recognizing and developing the soft skills within untapped talent, and by coaching untapped talent in the comfort-stretching process of becoming personally sound.

As a foundation for that discussion, however, we need to talk about organizational change from a higher-level view.

Plenty has been written about how organizations go through change, and there are all sorts of ways to successfully execute a planned changed process. Karen Wilhelm Buckley, an organizational development expert in California who is founder and codirector of The Wisdom Connection, cowrote an article/book chapter with me that outlines a seven-stage model of organizational change and transformation.[2] John Kotter, one of America's leading authorities on leadership and change, has an eight-step process for changing organizations. Let's not forget Tom Peters and Robert H. Waterman's "McKinsey 7-S" model that was made popular in their landmark book *In Search of Excellence, Lessons from America's Best Run Companies*, said by some to be the "greatest business book of all time."[3] All of these models are more than adequate to facilitate an organizationwide change processes.

Over the years, however, I have become partial to a change model that aligns with the issues in tapping untapped talent. This model is simple while still providing sufficient structure to design a change process that is thorough, flexible, and easily transferable to any organization's culture. It involves just three levels of organizational change.

Level One: The personal/internal. Change, even for organizations, begins with the individual. An organization, after all, is simply individuals who are grouped together. So this level addresses the factors you must consider as a leader about the individuals who will form the foundation of any meaningful, widespread change.

It starts with understanding the importance of what a person learns about himself during the change process—his values, beliefs, expectations, and worldview. This includes those things that are invisible and known only to the individual—or to you, personally, since you, as a leader, represent the first person who must buy into, adopt, and live the change.

Many of us make assumptions regarding what people believe or value, but we can't be 100 percent certain until we're told. This is the level of change that feeds our unconscious mind and acts as a trigger for our daily decisions and behaviors. It is where we explore our alignment with our organization within a personal context.

Organizations know they can't regulate what people believe or how they think, but they can regulate behavior. The challenge is when someone is in violation of a policy, such as that of sexual harassment. What generally drive such violations are the person's beliefs and values around women and power. Getting to the underlying issue is a journey through self-discovery. Leaders constantly need to be in this process so they can understand themselves, while also leading others through the process. And on the positive side, this self-discovery process opens the door to the hidden skills and talents that make you and those around you bloom.

This level of change also is where people discover and move past the blind spots (based on their filter systems) that prevent them from seeing new markets or innovative approaches to change.

In 1992, during my tenure as the director of diversity for the Bank of Boston, I gathered a group of executives to discuss the bank's opportunities in diverse markets. Everyone in the room was a white male except for me and Gail Snowden, an African American who was a senior leader with the bank.

After taking the group through several exercises that examined changing markets, Gail was the only one in the room who saw the possibility of generating revenue from community markets. Her counterparts couldn't comprehend how the bank could grow a business in low-income, urban communities with high concentrations of minority- and female-owned businesses. Building on concepts presented by her colleague Leon Wilson (another senior-level banker), Gail championed her idea, developed a business plan, and grew one of the most successful divisions in the bank. In fact, she became president of First Community Bank (a division of Bank of Boston). Her success exceeded anyone's expectations and the business model went national. Gail believed and knew what others at the table didn't—that people of color spent money, needed banking facilities in their communities, and were hard-working, reliable customers.

Gail's unique upbringing helped shape her understanding of the potential of this market. She grew up as the only child of Otto and Muriel Snowden, who founded Freedom House in 1949. The community-based nonprofit's mission is to "promote educational excellence, economic self-sufficiency community engagement and social justice in order to alleviate poverty in Boston's most distressed urban neighborhoods."[4] So Gail's life experience provided her the opportunity of witnessing firsthand the diverse working- and middle-class neighborhoods that were neglected by larger banks.

Mainstream banks across America have now settled in diverse communities and compete for the right to serve that customer base. That demographic represents big business opportunities. Still, in 2012, I continue to have similar conversations with top leadership—men (mostly) who are not from those communities and who have not had life experiences that broaden their belief systems.

The same scenario applies to untapped talent. Managers locked in a mental model of what a successful team member is or will be become committed to that model. They make their hiring, development, and promotion decisions based on the model. Most people hire in their image because they have grown to value the elements of success that made them successful. And why not, you might ask? Chris Matthews, the host of MSNBC's "Hardball," answered that question well at a luncheon I attended in July 2012: "If you have a problem and everyone in your inner circle is like you and there's no diversity, you're not going to get the best answer to your problem. Diversity provides different ways to examine a situation."

Consciously knowing who we are and how our worldview, values, beliefs, and expectations influence our decision-making is a critical part of being a leader. The more we participate in self-discovery and link our results to professional performance, the better the leader we'll emerge. That's why emotional intelligence is now one of the major soft skills leaders are expected to bring to their jobs and to coach throughout their teams.

Level Two: The interpersonal/external. Individual change is good, and the right place to start, but few of us work in a silo. And if we did, we wouldn't be concerned with organizational change. No, we work in groups—teams, herds, tribes,... whatever catch phrase you want to use. And groups function based on relationships. So it's at this level that we address how we (and others) build relationships and work with others.

If the personal/internal level of change is about the invisible, this level is all about what's visible to others. In many ways, it's where the organization comes to life—people, interactions, relationships, winning and failing together. It's the level that creates the combustible energy of an organization.

We establish rules, regulations, and, most important, norms on how people "should" behave when in the work environment. Our behaviors are observable by all and perceptions are made based on our behaviors. Colleagues assess each other's performances, determine informal and formal power lines, and decide whether someone "fits" in the team and organization. These types of factors feed the organizational culture and begin to establish in-group and out-of-group behavior.

Untapped talent can promote themselves out of the hidden workforce at this level of change, or they can languish. It largely depends on how they build relationships with others—how accurately they interpret their brand, reputation, and performance.

Too many people languish in the hidden workforce because they don't consider the collective influence of their peers on their success. Or, they haven't stopped to examine their alignment with their manager. Using 360-degree feedback tools can be an excellent method of assisting team members in building a shared reality regarding how they see themselves and how others see them.

Take John Michaels,[5] for instance. John was a successful executive in a large insurance company in Cleveland, Ohio, when his manager recommended he attend a top executive development program. John was excited about the opportunity to strengthen his leadership skills, but he was also curious about "why him." Frankly, he figured the training would be more helpful to one or two of his peers. John had been rated a strong performer in his division, and he was on several corporatewide projects that were extremely visible. He appreciated the chance to improve, but he felt he was doing great and that others needed this type of training more than he did.

During the first week of the program, however, John received feedback from a 360-degree assessment. The results were eye-opening. John discerned there was a major gap between how he viewed his relationships with his manager and with his peers. John thought those relationships were solid, but in both cases there were cracks that were keeping him from performing at his best and limiting his opportunities for advancement.

John had been with the company for years and had a strong relationship with the most senior-level executives, including the CEO. His manager, meanwhile, was relatively new to the organization. From the feedback, John realized that he often bypassed his manager when dealing with other executives. His manager felt left out of the loop on significant aspects of projects. He also felt like John wasn't helping him make and develop better relationships with the top leaders.

John's peers, meanwhile, gave him marginal scores on his teamwork abilities, even though John felt like he went out of his way to respond to their requests. John was startled by his results, but now he understood why some of the small, everyday interactions of work were more challenging than they should have been.

John's peers had quietly chosen not to inform John of their perceptions and would discreetly discuss John when he wasn't in the room. There were seeds of bitterness and envy over his successes, his opportunities for plumb assignments, and the way he communicated (sometimes with an air of superiority). His manager, meanwhile, had failed to provide hard performance-related feedback and had begun to keep John out of the loop on some projects in a passive-aggressive response to John bypassing him with senior executives.

John and everyone above and around him owned some responsibility for the situation. John couldn't change his peers' behaviors, but he could change his to the degree he felt was necessary. He wasn't going to change, however, until he had a more accurate view of reality.

It always surprises me when people don't consider the impact peers have on their success. Many people spend their time only managing up, and give little attention to the lateral relationships that interconnect with their success. Peers can unconsciously decide to derail a teammate's success. One person starts the drum roll and slowly but surely another and then another picks it up until the person is isolated, struggling, has lost all confidence, and slips into the hidden workforce or out the organization's door.

Level Three: The organizational. We bring our internal selves to work and it factors into our external relationships. The internal and external, in turn, shape the organizational decisions that we make for our teams and our companies. They shape our policies, our procedures, our price points, our products, our marketing, our hiring decisions...all of it.

So for organizations to change, leaders have to intervene on all three levels—they have to address the personal/internal, the interpersonal/external, and the nonpersonal/organizational.

When change reaches this third level, it has to consider the first two—and that loops the personal and interpersonal right back into the process. Level three is the culmination; it's where we apply our technical knowledge to create a difference for the organization, but it's also where our core values, beliefs, worldview, and relationships come into play to shape our work processes and business solutions.

Let me provide you with a couple of examples of how this can play out. I worked with a company that sells beauty-related products all around the globe. In emerging markets, the demographic of their primary customer base is a female from a lower economic class and of color. Yet because the product, marketing, and advertising decisions were made primarily by European leaders, the company was resisting new products specifically for darker skin tones and was using celebrities to endorse their products who looked more like Jessica Alba, Scarlett Johansson, or Taylor Swift than Halle Berry, Chen Hao, or Ildi Silva.

Thomas Stanton, author of *Why Some Firms Thrive While Others Fail*, points to research by Sydney Finkelstein, a professor with the Tuck School of Business at Dartmouth, that supports the idea that poor decisions often originate from unconscious bias. Finkelstein and his team researched and analyzed the decision-making of leaders of public and private organization, and found that "decision makers may be hampered by misleading experiences in their backgrounds (fighting the last war), misleading prejudgments, inappropriate self-interest, or inappropriate attachments, all of which can lead to flawed decisions."[6]

The organizational change required to identify and develop untapped talent happens only if you consider all three levels of organization change. All the levels are interconnected, but specific actions need to happen at each level to make an impact. So as a leader looking to mine that 70 percent with greater efficiency and success, you have to discern what you must achieve at each of the levels for you to maximize the performance of your organization. But you have to do that with an understanding of how the levels fit together.

The next three chapters cover strategies that come into play at each of the levels and, at times, at different levels at the same time. We'll start with creating a culture of talent stewardship, then we'll cover the interpersonal "soft" skills needed for success, and after that we'll look at the process of becoming "personally sound" and how self relates to work.

For organization change processes to be successful, they must take into consideration the culture of the organization. Executing a change on tapping untapped talent is no different. The subtle nuances of an organization culture will either support the change or inhibit its success. So we will explore organizational culture and what it means to build a culture of talent stewardship.

The soft skills of untapped talent often are hidden in personal values and show up most in external relationships. So we'll look at what those key soft skills are, why they often go hidden in the talent around you, and how to spot and cultivate those skills in people you might not expect.

The process of becoming personally sound is critical because it opens the doorways to change at all three levels. This is where you and your teams do the hard work of discovery—you discover who you are, how others see you, and how those things shape the skills you have and the decisions you make.

CHAPTER 5
The Culture Catapult

This page intentionally left blank

Building talent and culture will have the most significant, longest-lasting impact on an organization—more so than any other activity a CEO can do.

—John R. Strangfeld, chairman and CEO,
Prudential Financial

A few years ago the American Society for Training & Development (ASTD) felt compelled to define the term "talent management."
Why? Because the association's research determined there was no standard definition for a phrase that people in business had been using for decades. So, in a 16-page white paper released in 2009, ASTD presented the following definition for talent management: "An organizational approach to leading people by building culture, engagement, capability, and capacity through integrated talent acquisition, development, and deployment process that are aligned to business goals."[1]

Now close your eyes and say that definition out loud three times.

Clearly that very formal definition is more than a mouthful. That's because, well, it's a "formal" definition. It was carefully crafted, precise, and comprehensive, and all of that makes it overly academic for widespread use. If you're responsible for creating a talent management system in your organization, of course, you could start by breaking down and studying that definition. It would serve you well.

If you prefer something a little simpler and far easier to remember, however, then I'd go with ASTD's *description* of effective talent management: "[P]utting the right employee with the right skills in the right position at the right time."[2]

Right on. That's how you access untapped talent.

If a talent management system isn't "putting the right employee with the right skills in the right position at the right time," then it's not working. Of course, it sometimes takes a sophisticated system to accomplish that outcome. One that takes an organizational approach. One that builds culture, engagement, capability, and capacity. One that integrates talent acquisition, development, and deployment processes. And one that is aligned to business goals.

The rise of such sophisticated, highly integrated talent management systems speaks to the importance organizations are putting on people. But most of these systems, as important as they are, focus on managing talent that's already tapped. In other words, they focus on recruiting, developing, and retaining the talent that's traditionally been identified based on the unconscious biases ingrained in the organization's culture toward that particular group of high performers.

For your organization to discover and grow the untapped talent among its ranks—for you to fully tap into your team's talents—the leaders at every level of your organization must accomplish something that sounds simple but takes a great deal of time and effort: Cultivate a culture of talent stewardship. That's the foundation for *sustainable* talent management that goes beyond the obvious and taps into an organization's untapped talent.

The Culture of Talent Stewardship

"Culture" is a fascinating word because it carries multiple meanings that fit neatly together in an interesting way. As a verb, it can mean "to grow" or "to cultivate." And as a noun, it can refer to the behaviors and beliefs of a group. So when you think of them together, you get a picture of something (the noun) that has to grow (the verb) to stay alive.

In other words, a culture that's not growing is dying.

Unfortunately, all too many organizations fail to fully support a culture of talent stewardship, so they fail to fully tap into the talent that's available to them. They fail not because they don't value "culture" but because they miss the most important part of developing a culture—the parts that are invisible. And the cost of such failings is significant to a business's productivity and bottom line.

Edgar Schein, a former professor at MIT's Sloan School of Management, has significantly contributed to the study of organizational development, but he's perhaps best known for his model describing organizational cultures. Schein identified three distinct levels—artifacts, espoused values, and basic assumptions—that are based on the degree to which an observer can see them in an organization's culture.

Artifacts are easily identifiable elements like furniture or the dress code or the types of jokes people tell. When you visit someone's office for the first time, you notice these artifacts because you can see, hear, or feel them—you notice, for instance, if all the men are wearing coats and ties, whether the office furniture looks like it came from a second-hand store, or if the photos on the walls are portraits of former CEOs or candid shots of employees and their families.

Espoused values are what the organization officially professes to be. They are the stated rules, values, and philosophies. These show up in places like the company's website, the employee handbook, or a nicely framed poster in the office lobby. At Sam's Club, for instance, associates wear a lanyard that holds their ID and a card that says,

What Our Members Want
+
Clean, Fast, Friendly Clubs and Knowledgeable Associates
+
Growing, Retaining and Attracting Members
=
The Fastest-Growing Brand in the Warehouse Channel

The espoused values of a culture often are more general and high-level—a code of conduct, for instance, or list of values that says something like, "we value innovation" or "integrity matters." In most cases, they begin with conscious decisions by the leaders at the top—often from a founder—and are intentionally pushed down and through the organization.

Basic assumptions are unconscious behaviors that are so deeply ingrained that they're taken for granted and hard to recognize from within the culture. These evolve over time based on things like the personalities, perceptions, and interactions of the people within the organization.

They result from patterns that develop in response to problems or opportunities, and they can thwart or support espoused values. So, for instance, a company might have espoused values promoting risk-taking and innovation. But it also might have several layers of management reviewing projects, and each layer of management might have a history of stripping away some of the risky elements of an idea until what's left is the status quo. The cool, edgy, innovative approach ends up simple, safe, and ordinary. The pattern of "we love risks, just not that risk" responses from leaders unintentionally creates a culture that sends a different message: play it safe.

It's in this arena of a corporate culture that leaders have to move beyond talent management systems, because the greatest talent management systems in the world are doomed if the culture doesn't support them—not just with the artifacts and espoused values but with the oh-so-hard-to-control assumptions.

In most organizations, even those with sophisticated talent management systems and great intentions, talent stays untapped because the culture works against it. Instead of promoting growth, the culture becomes one of the "inhibitor environments" that we covered earlier. Those environments leave talent devalued and untapped. A strong culture of talent stewardship, however, provides an organic setting for identifying and growing the talent that goes untapped in other organizations.

Lisa Brooks Greaux, Ed., has worked in talent development for more than 20 years and now is head of Learning and Development for Pfizer Animal Health. She put it simply and accurately in our conversation on this topic: "The environment you put people in makes all the difference in the world."

If people are in an environment that supports what they want to do and helps them grow and impact the organization, Brooks said, they're much more inclined to give everything they've got to help the organization succeed.

"I have to know that even if I fail I'm not going to be fired, that I'll be OK," she said. "It's about creating that environment where I can take risks. It doesn't mean I take risks that aren't calculated—that I just go bet the farm. It means I'm going to take judicious risks, but if that risk, for whatever reason, doesn't work, well I'm not going to be penalized or demoted or made an example of."

Creating that type of culture requires more than well-crafted policies or pretty banners in the lobby of the home office, and it also goes beyond the things that are measured in a leader's performance review.

"It's one thing if I'm promoting something because I'm going to be measured on it on my performance appraisals," Brooks said. "It's another thing for people to do it even if it's not a metric. Anybody can put it in their corporate mission statement. It's quite another thing to see it in action."

In other words, a culture of talent stewardship begins with the informal practices of its leaders. These leaders take the time to get to know people throughout their organizations, not just those within their immediate sphere of influence. They encourage risk-takers by rewarding them when they succeed and helping them up when they fail. They act as informal coaches to the talent they spot, and they go to bat for people who otherwise wouldn't get a shot at a stretch assignment or promotion. And their behaviors help create a culture in which everyone around them values talent—a culture with established norms and a sense of consistency on how talent is viewed and how it is developed.

Let's look more closely at what you, as a leader, need to do if you're going to create this culture of talent stewardship—a culture that naturally identifies and grows talent that's waiting to get tapped.

Leaders Who Develop a Culture of Talent Stewardship Invest the Time to Know the Talent within Their Organization

You identify and then grow untapped talent by first getting to know people and assessing their talents—starting with their strengths, challenges, aspirations, and family environments. The first two deal with their abilities to perform; the last two impact motivation and provide the insights you need when you are managing and leading talent.

Brooks believes a leader should spend no less than 40 percent of his or her time in relationship-building activities. I agree. That includes coaching people, formally and informally, as well as observing them as they interact with other people. But mainly it's just about talking to people and getting to know them. It's about stopping for a few minutes at someone's desk and visiting, asking the second and third questions, and then remembering what you learned so you can follow up the next time you pass by.

"If I'm sourcing for talent 40 percent of the time," managers often ask me when I bring up this standard, "when do I have time for my real job?"

Your "real job" involves sourcing people, I respond. It's not "in addition to" your projects, making your numbers, worldwide travel, or team meetings. Developing teams, coaching and mentoring younger executives who demonstrate potential—it's all part of the way you should be working. You don't build relationships and source talent *at the expense* of other tasks; you do it as *a part* of almost all your tasks.

Some days, or even weeks, you may not have many opportunities to directly source and develop talent. You might be limited to a few side conversations before or after meetings. Other weeks you'll find time on the calendar for more formal, intentional relationship building. But you get to that 40 percent number by making relationships—and, thus, talent sourcing—a skill that's practiced naturally. Once you develop the skills, they become ingrained in your management and leadership style. Then you begin to see the benefits of knowing the talent that's in the environment. You remember that Michele Lee in research produced a comprehensive report for you on a very short deadline. You think, "I wouldn't mind having her on my team." And when the right situation comes up, Michele comes to mind. You slowly build mental files for the people you know and work with—adding names, learning about the skill levels attached to those names, and considering when you might use them or mention their abilities to others. You develop a reputation as a talent spotter, for your own teams and for the organization. And the more you build that reputation, the more others come to you with that expectation. People want to work with you. They want to show you what they can do. They want to share the very information you need to know about them.

All of that from investing your time into the lives of the people around you. From talking to them. From listening to them. From getting to know the untapped talent around you.

"That's really how you get to know people and understand the experiences they've had and how they think about the business," Brooks said. "Yes, it's up to people to get themselves out there and have some skin in the game (commitment/ownership), but it's incumbent on the leader to be sourcing talent all the time. That's part of what a leader should be doing."

At one regional company in the Midwest, for example, new general managers are trained through an in-the-field program that takes four–six months. District managers are expected to keep up with these trainees and check on them whenever they visit the locations where the trainees are working.

So district managers sometimes get an email from their boss, a vice president, that simply says, "Tell me how the trainees in your district are doing?" If they respond quickly, the VP knows they've been investing time in the lives of the trainees. If it takes several days, the VP knows they probably had to do some research just to remember the trainees' names.

Leaders who develop a culture of talent stewardship know the names of the talent within their organization. And they know much, much more. They take the time to learn the hidden gems of information—like a person's hobbies, background, interests, and nonwork experiences—that often prove invaluable when it's time to help people into the more formal talent pipelines.

This starts with informal conversations, but it evolves into more intentional coaching and one-on-one discussion where team members discuss how they fit into the department's goal, discuss their aspirations, and talk through their long-term goals.

All of these discussions, formal and informal, will give you a fuller sense of the talent—their technical skills, as well as their soft skills. It helps you discover the all-important "why" behind behaviors you see (or don't see) in people. It helps you understand how to motivate different people.

Not long ago I had breakfast with a chief diversity officer from a large medical distributor on the West Coast. We were discussing a course that was being held in the next building for emerging leaders, and she shared a story about a manager who frequently asked his direct reports questions about how they spent their weekends, how their family was doing, and what nonwork activities they enjoyed.

One of his employees, a young Latino woman I'll call Maria, would answer but reluctantly. She couldn't quite understand her manager's need for this information. She felt it was invading her privacy; she was there to work, not discuss her social life. Eventually Maria found an opportunity to ask her manager why he was so intent on "knowing her business." The manager was puzzled at first, and then realized what she was asking. "Oh," he said, "the more I know about you both professionally and personally, the more it helps me understand what motivates you, what assignments you might enjoy that may not be apparent based on your work history."

Then he told her a story about one of his previous direct reports.

"A couple of years ago I had a young middle manager working for me who was a gifted programmer," he said.

> Everyone raved about her computer skills, and she was progressing through the company without incident. On a business trip, over dinner,

I learned that she wrote short stories as a hobby and belonged to several community writing groups. Her business writing was always perfect, but I never imagined she enjoyed creative writing. Actually, her fiction writing was as good if not better than her computer skills. We talked for a long time about what she would like to do next in her career. It turned out she wanted to go into the communications department. And with her flair for writing, why not?

Maria slowly began to understand her manager's inquisitiveness. And while she remained guarded in what she shared, she noticed she didn't have the same resentment over his questions, that her relationship with her manager was getting better, and that she felt more a part of the team.

Your commitment to a deeper understanding of who people really are promotes collaboration at all levels. For instance, it generates buy-in—a willingness among people to engage in projects and to support work that is planned to move the organization forward. Yes, positional power can initiate a project, but relationships often move projects through the organization and across the finish line. Plus, demonstrating that you care for the whole person and not just the performer deepens their commitment to you as a leader and manager. Remember, people leave managers not companies.

Leaders Who Develop a Culture of Talent Stewardship Take a Nontraditional Approach with Their High-Performance Teams

Great leaders create high-performing teams so that they can harness that energy for something special. They bring people together, encourage them, guide them, support them, and provide them with space and an opportunity to grow and succeed.

"Leading through Connections," a study released in 2012 by IBM that's based on conversations with more than seventeen hundred chief executives in 64 countries, found that "collaboration is the No. 1 trait" that CEOs want in their employees.

"CEOs have a new strategy in the unending war for talent," the report said. "They are creating more open and collaborative cultures—encouraging employees to connect, learn from each other and thrive in a world of rapid change."

Research indicates that homogeneous teams—those with members who are similar to each other—communicate well, work well together, enjoy their work, and experience positive results. On the downside, these teams aren't as creative, aren't challenged from within, and don't experience much personal growth. On the other hand, heterogeneous teams—those with a broader mix of people—display more creativity, better problem-solving abilities, and greater personal growth. But they don't always communicate well or work well together, and their turnover rate can be high.³

As heterogeneous team members discover common ground, however, they can become more and more cohesive. And homogenous teams, given the right direction, can display amazing creativity. So with the right leadership, either style of team—homogeneous or heterogeneous—can become a high-performance team. But in my experience, heterogeneous teams are more likely to tap previously untapped talent, allowing it to shine and become more productive.

Let's say you work for a technology company and you need a team to work on a project that requires some creativity and forward thinking. You might lean toward a team full of 20-somethings known for their free-spirited approaches to life. You might not pick the woman with a military background (too rigid in her thinking) or the guy in his forties (not hip enough). If so, your team would have some holes because it would lack a diversity of experiences.

Apple founder Steve Jobs recognized this reality as far back as the mid-1990s.

"Creativity is just connecting things," he told *Wired* magazine.

> When you ask creative people how they did something, they feel a little guilty because they didn't really *do* it, they just *saw* something. It seemed obvious to them after a while. That's because they were able to connect experiences they've had and synthesize new things. And the reason they were able to do that was that they've had more experiences or they have thought more about their experiences than other people.
>
> Unfortunately, that's too rare a commodity. A lot of people in our industry haven't had very diverse experiences. So they don't have enough dots to connect, and they end up with very linear solutions without a broad perspective on the problem. The broader one's understanding of the human experience, the better design we will have.⁴

By creating a culture with diverse experiences, leaders can identify untapped talent and begin to grow those people who previously were stuck in their work. And the more they identify and grow that talent, the more they support a culture of talent stewardship. And the more that happens, the better the results for their business.

Charles Bolden, NASA's administrator (the equivalent of the CEO), in a video for IBM's Institute for Business Value, explained why it takes a diverse organization to solve complex problems:

> If we take a homogeneous group of people and ask them a question, I can guarantee you I'm going to get one answer. And I can't use one answer. The problems that we encounter...if we don't have diversity in thought, then we're just not going to be able to tackle the real critical, challenging questions that we have.[5]

Leaders Who Develop a Culture of Talent Stewardship Look Broadly, Look Deeply, Look Externally, and Look Often

The untapped talent in your organization isn't sitting right in front of you waving its arms to get your attention. To find it, you have to look across business lines, geographic locations, functions, and technical areas. You have to move outside of your comfort zone and look two to three levels down and across in the organization if you're going to broaden your perspective on who is in the organization.

Edward Lawler, director of the Center for Effective Organizations at the University of Southern California, estimates that senior managers should spend 30–50 percent of their time on talent management. As discussed earlier, this can be a scary number in our results-driven business environment, but it can lead to high-performing teams and a very strong bench for succession planning. Reaching out requires a curiosity to engage with others in light of, and a full knowledge of, the business direction of the organization and your team's specific goals.

Identifying untapped talent means getting out of your comfort zone. Remaining in a fixed environment and continuing to look in the same old places for talent won't help you identify new, fresh talent. It only adds to the status quo.

As you look broadly across business lines, functional and technical areas, and geographic locations, your peripheral view has to extend to lengths that you've yet to imagine. You can't allow the sea of people in your daily interactions to block your sightlines. They may be very good at what they're doing, but they may not be the answer to tomorrow's business challenge. Knowing where to find that future talent at a moment's notice could make the difference in your team's success and, therefore, the success of the organization.

Looking deeply involves knowing who is coming behind you. Leaders typically manage "up" the organization but seldom take time to consider who's behind them. Sometimes the person behind you is your next manager or the next answer to a complex business decision.

I recommend that senior leaders stay exposed to people at least two levels below them in the organization. This helps in several ways. Future leaders began to have contact with senior leaders and acquire a mental model of what leadership looks like for the organization. And as a leader, you begin to understand the depth of talent that exists in the organization so you can begin promoting that talent.

Looking external is about more than recruiting from outside your organization; it's about finding the untapped talent that is all around you all the time. It's about expanding beyond your corporate environment by keeping an eye on people you work with on external task forces, on community and civic projects, on boards, or in sporting outings.

Broadening your perspective on where you can spot and recruit talent increases your team's effectiveness. You bring in new ways of thinking and new ways of working when you hire from outside. It then becomes your responsibility to ensure that the added value of a diverse perspective is not lost in the cultural norms of an organization.

Finally, look often, because this is essential to building a strong pipeline. Many talent management processes are based on a performance management system. While a formal talent management process is critical to a company's success, it can't manage the daily talent decisions that leaders must make. The search for talent should be a continuous process—a natural part of a leader's style and way of working.

Leaders Who Develop a Culture of Talent Stewardship Eliminate Their Assumptions

Earlier we looked at some common assumptions—unconscious biases and implicit associations—and why they come about within the best-intentioned leaders. To identify and grow the talent in your organization, you have to become sensitive to these assumptions so you can eliminate them.

Your game-changer may be the unexpected hire or reassignment. You'll miss great opportunities to develop people if you make assumptions about their abilities because of organizational folklore or because they look different or because they haven't been in the role you're considering them for.

How do you eliminate these assumptions?

For starters, don't try to do it alone. Ask for advice and opinions from outside of your usual circle of confidants.

Second, take the time to come up with "what if" scenarios so that you can act quickly when the need arises. For instance, you might have to consider: What would we do if we expanded rapidly and needed different skills on the team? What if several of my high performers were recruited by competitors? Or what if I had an international assignment to fill and needed local talent to do so? How would I source the talent to ensure I examine all possibilities?

Third, remember that opposing voices aren't always troublemakers. Often they are creative people who have different filters and see situations from different perspectives. Appreciate their different perspectives and the value they can add to your team. Scott Anthony, author of *The Little Black Book of Innovation*, says these are the people who most naturally display the behaviors that generate innovation, but they are easily marginalized or overlooked.[6]

"Most organizations have people who follow these behaviors—even if they aren't immediately obvious to senior leadership," Anthony says. "Frequently they are what software entrepreneur Donna Auguste affectionately dubs 'aliens.' They don't quite fit the establishment, and that's exactly what you want."[7]

Fourth, look beyond the mirror.

Introspection is good. So to identify untapped talent, you start by understanding your own talents. But you can't let your attributes define what would add value to your team. Indeed, an entire team that looks and works "just like you" isn't likely to accomplish much more than you could accomplish on your own. You'd have more horsepower, but not much creative juice.

Start by understanding yourself and your role, and then develop a deep understanding of the people around you. This will help you look for people who are different and who can fill in the gaps of knowledge, skills, or who simply think in ways that will help open you and your team up to new ideas and will help you achieve your business goals.

Finally, don't judge; it's the easiest way to shut down budding talent.

Leaders Who Develop a Culture of Talent Stewardship Create New Opportunities and Stretch Assignments

Talent grows stale if it continues to perform the same duties year in and year out. Make it a point to rotate people through positions so they broaden and deepen their skills.

This requires taking some measured risks—allowing opportunities for success and nurturing people through the inevitable setbacks. It also requires an investment on your part. You have to provide direction, encouragement, and, at times, some tough-love feedback on their performance. The upside is that you can see people in new or different environments, perhaps using skills and talents you never knew they had.

If you are a senior executive, actively support your colleagues. Advocate for, protect, and fight for their career advancement. The organizational benefits include increased pipeline strength, enhanced employee engagement, and a stronger culture of talent stewardship.

Leaders Who Develop a Culture of Talent Stewardship Provide Nonmonetary Rewards

People respond to monetary rewards in certain situations, but mostly when it involves routine tasks, not when it involves creativity. Finding the untapped talent in your organization and getting the most of it, therefore, won't happen by throwing money at them or the situation.

All sorts of research support this. For instance, a Conference Board study asked employees what they expected from their employers, and "money" came in at the eighth position on the list. No. 1 was "interesting, challenging work," followed by "open, two-way communications," and "opportunities for growth and development."[8]

Look for ways to reward up-and-coming talent with atta-boys and atta-girls, especially in group settings; by providing opportunities for exposure to new challenges and to other leaders in the organization, by allowing them to take part in and present during cross-functional meetings and external conferences; by involving them on a highly visible taskforce; and by nominating them for the company's leadership training.

Adrian Gostick and Chester Elton, authors of *All In*, combed through a global research study of three hundred thousand people by Towers Watson and determined that the highest performing cultures have three common elements. The employees are engaged, enabled, and energized. These organizations, they say, have E + E + E cultures.

"These E + E + E cultures saw average annual operating margins twice as high as organizations with just high employee engagement and three times higher than those with low engagement," the authors wrote. In other words, "The best managers ensure their people are engaged, enabled and energized, which leads to much greater business results."[9]

That's because those cultures provide rewards that go beyond the financial and that allow talent to emerge from the hidden workforce and bloom to its true potential.

Creating a culture of talent stewardship is about long-term gain. It must be viewed as a process and not an event. It must be embraced by leaders as a way of working so that it's not personality driven and so that it will withstand changes of leadership and business cycles. It's in the interest of every organization to grow and hire great talent but, more importantly, to create an environment where talent is viewed as a valuable resource in today's demanding business world.

LEADERSHIP EXERCISE: ASSESSING YOUR TALENT CULTURE

Do you promote a culture of talent stewardship? Assess your ability to build a culture of talent stewardship by taking the short quiz here. It should help you determine your strengths and areas for improvement in building a strong culture of talent stewardship. Remember, building culture is a process not an event. Allow time for new behaviors and attitudes to take place.

Step 1. Check the statement that best describes your skills and abilities in talent stewardship.

1. I execute talent stewardship at my corporation/organization.
2. I spend time getting to know people and understanding their career aspiration.
3. I know people based on the work assignments I manage or participate in.
4. I spend between 30 and 50 percent of my time identifying talent.
5. I'm conscious about looking for talent inside, outside, or across the organization.
6. I have hired people with views different than my own.
7. I seek to provide new opportunities and stretch assignments for my team.
8. I advocate for others who are not on my team but demonstrate great skill.
9. I reinforce good performance with public acknowledgments, additional days off, or assignments on task forces.
10. I have more to learn about talent stewardship.

   Scoring: Each check is worth 10 points for a total of 100.
   70 and above = you're strong as a steward of talent
   59–69 = needs focused work
   58 and below = should consider getting a coach to assist with skill building

Step 2. Have your team and others rate your talent stewardship.
Assess the gap between the scores.
Develop an action plan for improvement.

This page intentionally left blank

CHAPTER 6

The Serendipitous Soft Skills of Tapped Talent

This page intentionally left blank

One aspect of serendipity to bear in mind is that you have to be looking for something in order to find something else.
—Lawrence Block, mystery novelist

Have you ever wondered about the difference between a solid performer and a superstar performer?

You might assume it's mainly about the person's technical ability. Well you'd be partly right. Technical skills, knowledge, and ability are important to superstars, but there are other success factors that go beyond task performance—soft skills.

Competence with soft skills, in fact, is essential even to entry-level success in more and more organizations. According to a 2006 study, the most critical skills employers want in *new employees* are things like "professionalism/work ethic, oral and written communication, teamwork/collaboration and critical thinking/problem solving."[1] More recent surveys, including several by websites that focus on helping graduates find jobs, confirm this trend. A study released in 2012 by Millennial Branding and Experience Inc. found that employers see communications skills (98 percent), a positive attitude (97 percent), and teamwork skills (92 percent) as "important or very important" to entry-level jobs.[2]

These and other soft skills only grow in importance as we move up the organizational charts. Superstars have the full package; they bring all of the technical skills, but they also excel in the soft skills. Excellence, not just competence, in soft skills is what distinguishes them from other players.

In fact, it's the soft skills that are the greater predictor of success in life. In "The Illinois Valedictorian Project," Karen Arnold tracked the success of 81 high-school valedictorians and salutatorians for ten years following their graduation. She found that almost all excelled in college, but only one in four were at the highest professional levels when compared to non-high-school valedictorians of similar age and profession. The difference? The more successful ones were not only academically smart, but also excelled in soft skills.[3]

These skills can look different in different organizations, but they typically involve self-awareness, cultural competence, emotional intelligence, political savvy, interpersonal skills, executive presence, and leadership ability.

These soft skills often become significant blind spots in the development of untapped talent. The nontangible nature of the skills makes it difficult for some people to recognize their importance in daily operations. It's easy to dismiss soft skills as those "things some people are born with and others, like me, are not." It can be hard to define soft skills or to get a grip on what "improvement" looks like in these areas.

We often know soft skills when we see them, or when they're missing in someone (not us), but we also know they look different for different people.

For one person, they may show up as an ability to remain calm in difficult situations. For another, it's a strong presence that's accented by superb communication skills. For someone else, it's an ability to listen, learn, and guide a group through a difficult project. And for yet another person it involves paying careful attention to what needs to be done and then doing those things.

Many emerging executives are dumbfounded when they realize that their intelligence and technical skills—the things that put them on their initial path to success—aren't enough to get them to the next levels of success. When their soft skills are weak or missing, most people will languish or move at a slower progression than their counterparts. They don't understand it. They blame others. They get frustrated. They grow cynical. And they slip into the hidden workforce, where many of their greatest talents will go untapped.

A Budding Talent

To better understand the power and impact that comes when someone makes exceptional use of soft skills, let me introduce you to Wayne Budd, a lawyer, businessman, and community leader.

Wayne began his career without what you may consider a spectacular pedigree. His mother and father (an ex-Marine turned police officer in Springfield, Massachusetts) emphasized education, and Wayne did well in school. He went to Boston College for his undergraduate degree in economics, and then to Wayne State University for law school. He worked for Ford Motor Co. by day and attended classes at night, graduating in 1967. That was enough to land him an entry-level job as an attorney with the city of Boston, but he was far from a superstar in the making. He was simply another smart, young guy with a law degree looking to make a go of it in Boston.

With no large law firms chasing his services, he cofounded his own with high-school friend Thomas Reilly, but Budd & Reilly began with very few clients and the partners made very little money.

So Wayne entered the early career stage of his life with a sharp mind, a solid work ethic, and some natural gifts for relating well with other people. But his considerable talents easily could have gone untapped. Instead, he identified and developed some critical soft skills that helped him excel.

It started when mentors took him under their wings and helped him grow personally and professionally. Wayne points out that he knew very few business and community leaders when he returned to Boston following law school, so he had to get involved in activities that helped him develop those connections. As he developed relationships with business and community leaders, they saw things in him that he often didn't see himself and gave him opportunities to thrive in a variety of industries and roles.

"There were some guys around town who really helped me, who got me on track," he said. "They went out of their way. They said, 'I don't know what I see in you, but I see something. Let me help you.' I got up on their shoulders."

What they saw in Wayne but couldn't articulate was the development of a set of soft skills that he himself credits with his career success. And to Wayne's credit, he embraced their help. Too often, untapped talent stays untapped because they are unwilling to seek and take the advice of others. They lack the confidence, they can't get past their pride, or they don't know how to ask for help, so they go it alone and, therefore, don't go very far.

Wayne became "tapped" talent because he learned how to build relationships and teams, to get things done, to make everyone feel important, to smooth the edges of difficult conversations, and because he figured out how to spot the untapped talent around him so that they could become part of the rising tide that lifts the organizational ship.

Budd's law firm eventually grew, took on new partners, and became the largest minority-dominated firm in New England. The firm, perhaps best known as Budd, Wiley, & Richlin, attracted and developed talented young attorneys who eventually became prominent in the East Coast legal community. For instance, some of the talent he attracted included Steven Wright, current executive partner for Holland & Knight's Boston Office (a 135-lawyer office of a national law firm); Ralph Martin, General Counsel Northeastern University and former Boston Suffolk County district attorney; and Fletcher (Flash) Wiley, former president, Greater Boston Chamber of Commerce, board member of TJX Corporation, and a national-level businessman.

Wayne, meanwhile, went on to become US attorney for Massachusetts and associate attorney general of the United States. He was president of Bell Atlantic's New England division, executive vice president and general counsel of John Hancock Financial Services, and a senior partner with the Goodwin and Procter law firm. And none of that includes his work as a member of corporate and nonprofit boards, or the fact that he served as the first African American president of a state's bar association (Massachusetts).

Oddly, when Wayne describes his career advancements, he tosses out phrases like "purely serendipitous" and "happenstance." He doesn't deny that he did his part to be in the right places at the right times with the right skills. He just doesn't link his personal accomplishments to an overwhelming supply of personal talent and ambition, and he graciously acknowledges the forces outside his control that often worked so conveniently to his advantage.

Wayne's soft skills helped him become much more than a successful attorney—they helped him become a great leader. A superstar. And the fact that his talents didn't go untapped should serve as an encouragement to the rest of us, because the hidden workforce is full of workers who have or can develop the very skills that made Wayne so successful.

Other people spotted those skills in Wayne and helped him tap into them. He, in turn, learned to spot these skills in others and to help those people tap into them. His story, therefore, provides lessons for all of us about these serendipitous skills, how to identify them in ourselves and in others, and how to tap them.

Spotting the Soft Skills

Wayne developed soft skills that made him valuable as a leader at every stop in his career, and those are the skills he looks for when spotting untapped talent in others.

These skills made him a valuable asset in financial services even though he had no experience in financial services. They made him coveted by a telecommunications company even though he knew nothing about telecommunications. They got him recruited to government law to oversee areas in which he'd never practiced. And they landed him in one of the nation's top legal firms even when he had no portfolio of clients.

Spotting untapped talent (in yourself and in others) isn't about finding the hard skills specific to a particular task or position. It's about finding and developing the soft skills that work in any and every environment. These are the skills that ultimately can get untapped talent out of the hidden workforce. These are the skills one needs to identify and cultivate for his or her own career and as a forward-thinking leader.

There's a baseline of skills that everyone needs for success, whether it's in law, medicine, science, education, finance, or any other industry or profession. After successfully developing those skills and gaining the right experiences, you consider the other factors that separate the capable from those who will excel. But unless the baseline is met, you're not sitting at the table.

As I noted at the start of this chapter, some really smart people often assume their intelligence is going to take them all the way to the top, but many of them reach a point of diminishing returns on that investment. And if that's all they've invested in—the intellectual intelligence but none of the emotional intelligence—then they'll get stuck or start a slide backward.

They can look like the introvert who sits quietly at a workstation all day, head down and task-oriented. Or they can look like the bull in a china shop who disrupts a meeting simply by walking in. Or the arrogant guy who is proficient in his work and has a high IQ but who people avoid because of his "the world centers around me" personality.

Of course, the smart and arrogant sometimes rise to the top of organizations and stay there, but that's taking the path of most resistance. Why not develop the soft skills that help you work well with others, accelerate the development of your workforce, *and* rise to the top?

The answer to those rhetorical questions is that there is no good reason for not developing your soft skills or for helping your team develop their soft skills so their talents can become more fully tapped. So let's take a closer look at these all-important soft skills.

In the Know

I mentioned earlier that soft skills typically involve self-awareness, cultural competence, emotional intelligence, political savvy, interpersonal skills, executive presence, and leadership ability. And under each category there are various behaviors that further define and describe soft skills. But if you want a more simple way to categorize them, consider these two big buckets: What you know and how you're known.

When I talk about *what you know*, I'm not talking about your formal education, your IQ, or your technical skills. Again those are the baseline abilities—the skills that get you into the game. You better have those, but they'll only get you so far. Then you better "know" the things that only come from your experiences—the things that come from paying attention to and learning from your experiences.

For instance, how well do you understand the culture of your organization or how quickly can you assess and understand the workings of a new team? Or what have you learned from life (not just from work) that you can apply to challenges and opportunities within your work?

These experiences very often come from deep within your background (where you grew up, your family dynamics, etc.), from seeking (and getting) work on a broad range of projects and types of projects, and from your extracurricular activities.

Wayne Budd, for instance, was quick to volunteer for committees and to chair them when possible. This is how he met future mentors and, later, those he could mentor. And this is how he learned how to sit in a room with people and get them to work together.

"Chairing a task force, being on a committee, being chairman of a non-profit—it really gave me confidence in my leadership, in my decision-making, in getting people to work together," he said. "That's as important as any other skill set."

What you know experientially helps you develop the right people skills and the contacts that can untap your talent.

How you're known reflects the soft skills connected to your reputation. How are you seen by your direct reports? By your supervisors? By people in other departments? By others in your industry? By clients? By vendors? What's your reputation in the community? What do people say about you when you're not in the room? In other words, what's your "personal brand"?

One reason John Hancock hired Wayne as its general counsel was because he had a solid reputation and the type of credibility needed as the organization moved from a privately held to a publically held company. The same was true with Bell Atlantic (now Verizon). Bell recruited him to serve as president of its New England Division because it needed a leader who would represent the company in a very public fashion.

At every stop, Wayne displayed his own skills and talents while building an impeccable reputation as a leader with excellent soft skills. And he looked for those same soft skills in the people around him—people he could trust, who worked hard, who said what they'd do and did what they said, who weren't afraid to say what they thought, who served others, and who reflected well on the organization.

"You really do have to have your reputation in good shape," he said. "You really have to have impeccable integrity. You have to be a person whose word is good and who is reliable. Your personal life is in order. You aren't going to embarrass me. That sort of reputation on a personal level separates you from others."

Those are the soft skills that show up in *what you know* and *how you're known*. Those are the talents others saw in Wayne and that they helped him tap into. And those are the talents he tapped in the people around him.

"To the extent that I've been successful," he said, "it's those kinds of things that have worked for me."

The Wind in Your Sails

The soft skills that you need to identify and develop in untapped talent are very much like the wind: You might not physically see them, but you can sense and feel their presence or their absence. With them, things move forward. Without them, things stall.

How do you "spot" things like courage, curiosity, agility, passion, or any of the other intrinsic traits that show up in people with strong soft skills? You look for them—all the time—in the way people behave when no one appears to be watching.

You notice when a team that was once malfunctioning has a new leader who has put it on track. What did the leader do? He or she may have used some technical expertise to establish credibility, but most teams are dysfunctional due to personality differences and working styles. The new leader was able to approach the project with a "soft" touch and move things forward.

So how do you know when someone can handle those types of situations?

Wayne shared his perspective:

I look around the room, and maybe I see how Mary Smith is interacting with her colleagues around the table. I watch how she greets the janitor. Or I notice how she treats a secretary. I see how she's thought of by others. Is she respectful or is it "me, me, me"? Then maybe I put her on a task force and see how she does, see how she gets things done.

Lisa Brooks Greaux, the executive at Pfizer I mentioned in a previous chapter, told me that she looks for people who are curious about the world in general, because those are the people who continually learn and grow. Their curiosity, if nurtured properly, produces creative solutions to some of business's biggest problems. They ask the "what if" questions and draw on a large bank of knowledge that comes from looking for answers just for the sake of learning new things.

"I look for someone who is curious about making things better," she said. "I want someone who is fundamentally interested in helping people reach their potential."

Lisa also values courage, because life isn't a smooth ride.

"I look for somebody who is courageous enough to say I'm willing to stand alone on this," she said. "They have deep-seeded believes in the work they want to do. There are times when you have to stand alone and say I believe in this so much I'm willing to risk this."

That courage must be tempered with mental agility.

"They believe deeply in what they believe in," Lisa said, "but they have the ability to recognize another perspective and see it for what it's worth."

Spotting these sorts of traits in rising stars isn't hard, but it's often difficult to see them in untapped talent. Untapped talent often hides from view and can look, at least in the work setting, somewhat passive and lacking in ambition. That's why you have to look beyond the obvious. If someone shows courage, curiosity, and agility in other aspects of life—with their families, their place of worship, as a volunteer, and so on—then that person will likely show courage, curiosity, and agility at work when given some direction and encouragement.

That's why it's critical to look for passion, even if it's not in something work related. If you can spot passion in someone, then you can start seeing the soft skills that relate to those passions. Let's say you start talking to a direct report and learn that he's passionate about improving the lives of children. That's why he volunteers with a group that provides programs for at-risk kids. From that, you begin seeing a great depth of self-awareness in this person, as well as his ability to work with people from different cultures. And you start seeing ways that those soft skills can directly apply to a project you're getting ready to launch.

One senior-level executive who oversees a team with international responsibilities put it this way: "The key to plugging into people's abilities is to talk to them about what they love and then try to assign them opportunities to do what they love. Because if they do what they love, you know what happens."

What happens, to quote Howard Thurman again, is that they come alive.

Here is an inventory of soft skills. It is not an exhaustive list by any stretch of the imagination, but it does provide greater clarity on what we mean by soft skills. Review the inventory and place a check by the soft skills you and your team members demonstrate. The empty boxes will provide the information on what needs improvement for you and your team. Remember soft skills vary by organization; add to the list to capture your organization's culture.

LEADERSHIP EXERCISE: TAKING A SOFT SKILLS INVENTORY

Skill	You	Team member	Team member	Team member	Team member	Team member
Self-Awareness—an understanding of yourself, your values, and what motivates your behaviors. • You have an accurate understanding of "self" and your values. • You have an awareness of your feelings and their connection to performance. • You are aware of your perceptions of others and others' perceptions of you. • You understand that your actions can have unintended consequences. • You can self-monitor your actions, mindset, and attitude while making corrective actions.						
Cultural Competence—the ability to work effectively across cultures. • You work effectively across cultures. • You accept multiple worldviews as legitimate perspectives. • You recognize your own biases and prejudices. • You have a genuine interest in learning about others.						

Skill	You	Team member	Team member	Team member	Team member	Team member
Emotional Intelligence—the ability to respond maturely to challenging situations. • You remain steady despite confusion and challenges. • You use life experiences to address unknown situations. • You are personally sound (you have a healthy sense of your life experiences).						
Political Savvy—the ability to read the nuances of an organization and act accordingly. • You have a radical temperament. • You display solid "corporate citizenship" (demonstrate engagement and loyalty). • You are knowledgeable about the formal and informal activities in an organization. • You move the organization's agenda forward over your own.						
Interpersonal Skills—an effective people person who works through others to obtain success. • You build strong relationships across the organization and in the larger community. • You network with ease and confidence. • You are interested in the success of others.						

Skill	You	Team member	Team member	Team member	Team member	Team member
• You work cooperatively with others. • You create a comfortable work environment						
Executive Presence—the ability to send a message of competence, confidence, and credibility.						
• Your personal brand is strong; others speak well of you even when you're not in the room. • You have strong verbal and written communication skills. • You dress appropriately for your organization. • Your confidence and self-image align with your abilities.						
Leadership Ability—the ability to successfully take responsibility.						
• You're a critical thinker with the ability to solve problems. • Your word is your reliability factor. • You advocate for others. • You express courage through risk-taking and conventions. • You show mental agility—an openness to change and other ideas.						

CHAPTER 7

Personally Sound: Tapping into Your Talents

This page intentionally left blank

> Why fit in when you were born to stand out?
> —Dr. Seuss, author

One of the first principles of consulting that professors drilled into my head when I entered the master's program in organizational development at Pepperdine University was that "the more personally sound you are, the better consultant you'll be."

At first, this only made intellectual sense to me. Later, after weeks of "T-groups"—sensitivity training where I got to know more about myself—the message about being "personally sound" truly began to sink in. Images of my life and the feelings attached to them kept coming up, and I didn't like everything I saw, nor was I comfortable with what I felt.

As I began the process of discovery, however, I slowly began seeing myself in a different light. I began to see strengths, courage, beauty, and intellect hiding behind a persona I created that projected confidence and authority. I slowly allowed myself to try new ways of thinking without fear of failure. I tapped into something I couldn't define at the time. Two things became a driving force for me: Learning more about myself and realizing that I needed to separate my personal and professional issues from my clients' challenges. It would be easy but not professional to transfer and project my inner thoughts, emotions, and perspectives onto my clients. I must be capable of maintaining objectivity during a coaching session, team building actvity, or analyzing results from an assessment. Understanding me is the key to achieving this mature level of self-awareness.

This type of deep, personal awareness is critical to effective leadership and it triggers positive business results. A report by the Korn/Ferry Institute put it this way:

> Study after study has found that self-awareness is a key factor associated with high performance and potential and an indicator of long-term career success, especially for leadership roles (Church 1997; Sala 2003). To be sure, leadership demands cognitive ability, motivation, experience, learning agility, and more. But when all things are equal, self-awareness appears to be the trait that best explains why some leaders succeed when others derail.[1]

When I coach senior executives through this process of discovery, we begin by reflecting on their families, their childhoods, and any significant experiences that helped shape their professional journeys. What we learn is that we carry many traits, skills, and abilities into our professional lives that emerged from our personal lives. Our professional self is shaped by our core values and beliefs. And while we may spend time at work controlling our behavior, that behavior is founded on our life experiences and has an impact on how we perform, how we interact, and what we achieve.

Becoming "personally sound" isn't just good advice for consultants and executives, it's foundational for anyone who wants to experience the value hidden in their untapped talents. The sooner we discover our untapped talents, the sooner we can put them to better use, but, equally as important, the sooner we can fully experience life because we can put away the parts of our histories that's held us down—personally, professionally, emotionally, or all three.

As leaders within an organization, part of our role is to help those around us become "personally sound" so that they can find their own hidden talents and make the most of their careers and lives. Helping the talent around them develop "personal soundness" allows them to really dig into their most hidden talents and make the most of them. But here's the catch: In order to recognize and develop the untapped talent in others, you have to recognize it in yourself—you have to develop your own personal soundness. So you might want to approach this chapter with bifocals, reading as a student who should go through the process for your personal benefit and as the mentor who will shepherd others through the process.

Getting to these untapped talents begins with a simple, but often difficult, three-step process. It starts with identifying our crucible moments. Then we must reflect on how those moments shaped us and where they are taking us. Finally, we reconcile ourselves with who we were, who we are, and who we want to become. Let's look at an example.

River of Life

Mallik Angalakudati stood in front of a flip chart, marker in hand. Images from the past 43 years zipped through his mind like a high-speed slideshow, each frame representing a milestone in his extraordinary journey.

He'd been given an assignment we call the "River of Life"—a short exercise to identify and discuss the crucible experiences that shape a person. The challenge came with a process; and, as an engineer, he thrived on process. So after giving the task some thought, he stepped toward the easel and began recreating the frames that stood out the most to him. He took his marker and sketched...

A river with several bends...
An airplane...
An Enron logo with cracks in it...

Several other people were in the room, each making their own drawings of their extraordinary journeys on their own sheets of flip-chart paper. Then, when everyone in the group finished their drawings, each took turns explaining the relevance of what each had drawn.

Mallik shared his story as if telling it—and hearing it—for the first time. He grew up in south India, he explained. His parents separated when he was six, so he and his brother lived with his mother, a teacher at a middle school, in a small home with his maternal grandparents. There were very few single-parent households in India in the 1970s, and a single woman raising children carried a negative social stigma. To avoid this, Mallik's mother chose to live with her parents.

The family fit in India's lower middle class, which meant they weren't poor but that their only hope for a better life was through education.

"You needed to be really good to get scholarships or financial aid for college," he later told me, "So my mom raised me with the unflinching focus on education."

The public schools weren't very good, and his family couldn't afford the private tutoring that wealthier children received. So Mallik, with the help of his mother, developed an amazing work ethic that helped him excel academically. When the time came for college, he applied to the prestigious Indian Institute of Technology (IIT)—India's version of MIT. Applicants from across the country take a test and only those who score in the top 2 percent win admittance. Mallik didn't get in the first year he applied, but the second year he made it.

With his education now mostly government funded, life got a little easier for Mallik. His father picked up his living expenses, and his education at IIT was essentially free. But he didn't slow down. He decided to come to the United States for postgraduate studies. His aunt in America loaned him $4,000 for airfare and his first year's expenses at the University of North Carolina (UNC), so he packed his bags and headed halfway around the world. Before he boarded his flight, his father approached him at the Mumbai airport and gave him a jacket and $20. "This is all the money I have," his father said. And when he took it, it became all the money Mallik had. Just before landing in the United States, Mallik, having spent $3 on a snack between flights in London, realized his financial situation might pose a problem once he arrived in the United States.

"What if my aunt doesn't meet me at the airport in America?" he asked himself nervously.

She did, of course. But there was an administrative problem with his acceptance at UNC, so Mallik spent a semester at Texas Tech University in Lubbock, Texas. When he finally made it to North Carolina, his first objective was simple: Stay there. "UNC admits the top 100 international students with a merit scholarship," he said, "but that's only for one year. The next year you are completely at the mercy of the sponsoring department. In 1991, there was limited funding. So the only way to ensure I got continued funding was to be No. 1 in my class."

Mallik dedicated himself to his studies, working 14–16 hours a day on keeping his scholarship. He limited his circle of friends and made little time for the fun most college students enjoyed. He earned the scholarship, plus another, and he left UNC with a master's in science with a focus on water resourcing engineering. He then spent three years working in Salt Lake City, Utah, before returning to school—this time at the University of Michigan—for an MBA.

When he finished that degree, Mallik had his choice of nine job offers, including one from Enron. At its peak, the Houston-based energy company impressed investors with its reported annual revenues of more than $110 billion. It seemed like a great opportunity, not to mention a chance to escape the cold of Utah or Michigan. With an offer in hand, he and his wife set out for Houston.

His hard work helped him climb the corporate ladder fast, and along with that came financial success. He and his wife had their first child, they paid down his student loans, took a vacation to Paris, bought a luxury car...times were good. Much of Mallik's savings went into Enron stocks that doubled every year. He figured he'd be a millionaire by age 40.

Then Enron imploded under the weight of one of the nation's biggest corporate accounting scandals. When it filed for bankruptcy in 2001, investors lost billions of dollars and employees like Mallik saw their pensions go as dry as the west Texas desert. In fact, Mallik lost his life's savings and investments—around $300,000—as well as his job. He and his wife, now pregnant with their second child, were left with a $4,500 severance package, less than $6,000 in a savings account, and an unsympathetic stack of bills.

"I never lost hope," Mallik said. "I did the only thing I could. I tried to get interviews lined up. Failure was not an option. Once I had an interview lined up, I would prepare all night learning everything I could about the company. There was no Plan B. I didn't sleep much for two weeks. But I got three offers, which wasn't easy back then. They weren't great offers, but they were a paycheck."

Mallik spent several years as a consultant for different companies before settling in at National Grid, an international gas and electricity company with a division that serves much of the northeastern United States. When the company made some changes and several people were laid off, Mallik survived in large part, he believes, because of the skills he'd learned during his journey. He had the technical skills and he knew how to work hard, but he also had learned valuable lessons about working well with others. Not only did that help him keep his job, but National Grid asked Mallik to lead an important strategic project.

"I'm a likeable guy, and I'm not into conflict," he said.

Enron was a very individualistic environment, but even back then I never tried to do things by myself. I got along with people. It was during my consulting career, however, that I became conscious of the value of working with others. I realized no matter how bright you are, your ability to accomplish things by yourself is very limited. So I went from being the likeable guy you enjoy having a beer with to making an intentional effort to work together with people so we could get things done. I had to grow that skill.

For Mallik, the "river of life" exercise helped expose some of his untapped talents—and some he'd been tapping without knowing it. He could see how his experiences across multiple cultures—from the unforgiving caste system of India, to the racial biases he encountered moving around the United States, to the climb and fall and restarting of financial successes—created in him a work ethic and resourcefulness that allowed him to use his considerable intellect for success. Fortunately for him, he had tapped into enough of those talents to grow his professional career to a high level.

Viewing those talents in a new light brought new energy to his career and life. Mallik had entered a danger zone that's common for many high performers. If they aren't intentional about moving forward in the right ways, they can become satisfied with success or get stuck in the status quo. Their talent can slide from tapped to untapped, even as they occupy a position of high authority. Mallik's look back into his past helped him prevent a possible slide into the hidden workforce.

"This is so liberating," he told me.

His reconciliation at that moment was coming to grips with his past. All he'd been focused on previously was moving forward and survival. "I never looked back at my life—at the skills I acquired and how they shaped me. I never understood that myself. Plus, listening to the other stories was amazing. I began viewing myself differently. I got plenty of breaks, and my suffering has been limited. Seeing the resilience of other people was humbling and inspiring."

Beverly Edgehill is the former executive director of The Partnership, the organization that sponsored the event where Mallik discovered the power of his story. She chose to use the "river of life" exercise after hearing the Hopi Indian proverb that says, "The one who tells the stories rules the world." Telling his story helped Mallik understand and take control of his world.

"Everything builds from our direct experiences," Beverly told me. "In our lives, we are building mental models based on our life experiences.

We must know we are more than the sum of our parts and our unique life experience shows itself at any moment in time."

Beyond the Crucible

Sometime around the fifteenth century, an unknown European entrepreneur discovered an alternate use for night lamps. If made correctly, these earthen bowls could withstand a high degree of heat and become melting pots for metals. They called them *corusible*, from the Latin *crucibulum*, but the word later morphed into what we use today: crucible. Its popular meaning morphed, as well. By 1645, people used *crucible* to refer to any severe test or trial—the human experience of being tested by the fires of life.

Untapped talents typically form within the crucible experiences of life—those challenges we've faced along the way that often, but not always, flow directly from our differences from the mainstream. A crucible experience is life-altering; it changes our attitudes, our behaviors, or both, and gives us a new perspective. It can shape us in positive and negative ways. A crucible experience can hit us with the immediate force of a lightning strike, as with the unexpected death of a loved one or friend, or it can stretch out over time, as with a series of subtle but connected events. Very often, crucible experiences involve both—a series of events that might seem insignificant and unrelated but that are brought together by a single, traumatic incident.

Kim,[2] a Chinese friend of mine who grew up in California, was raised by parents who presented consistent, unified reinforcements about the core value of family. Her dad encouraged her independent spirit, constantly challenging Kim to analyze events and draw her own conclusions. He challenged her to ask "why" questions about everything, so her belief in the importance of family was more than a nod to tradition—it was tested by her sharp, inquisitive mind.

Her crucible experience, therefore, revolved around the divorce of her parents when she was 15. It rocked her adolescent world, partly because divorce always rocks an adolescent's world but mainly because it ran counter to everything she'd been raised to believe.

The crucible experienced stretched on for years. She was closer to her father, so she lived with him until she heard her mother's "side of the story" and got into an argument over it with her dad. "He disowned me, saying I had betrayed him," Kim recalled. She ended up living with her grandparents, then with a friend, then on her own, then with her mother—all before she had graduated from high school. The anger she felt toward her father, meanwhile, shaped the woman, wife, mother, and professional she became—a serious individual with a keen mind but not always viewed as approachable.

Discovering our crucible experiences and getting something positive from them comes only from reflection, a self-discovery process where we find spaces in our lives to actively understand who we are, where we are, and where we are going. This includes telling our story as a method of uncovering strengths we didn't know we had. It challenges us to ask: What's the landscape of our situation? Who are the players? Did I do the best I could? How do I make it better next time? It creates a full conscious acceptance of our experiences, and it allows us to learn from failure.

This reflection can be planned or forced by circumstances. When my mom died, I didn't take any time off from work. I worked 18-hour days and focused on anything other than facing some hard questions about our relationship. It wasn't until nearly three years later when I took some time off between jobs that I reflected on who she was, what our relationship was, and the impact she had on my life. That reflection led to reconciliation.

Mom lived 89 years, and her life was filled with love, family, and her God. It took me the better half of my life to appreciate the grace and strength she carried, for I spent a great deal of my life trying very hard not to be who she was. We were always very close and connected by our common love for one another. But I couldn't appreciate the beautiful simplicity of her life, and she never understood, although always supported, why her daughter was drawn to a life so totally different from hers.

I didn't have children; she had eight. I sought the corporate arena; she was a practical nurse. I was spiritually focused; she was a devoted Christian raised by her father, a Baptist minister. She didn't start driving until she was in her forties; I got my license at 16, largely as a single act to control my life, my path, and my existence. She fancied being home, cleaning her house, taking care of her family, cooking, and visiting with her sisters; I've had a housekeeper for years, cook only when I am afforded the time to do so, and enjoy pursuing adventure.

My mother was happy with a few thousand dollars in the bank and a mortgage-free house. Her life's dream was to have a beautiful home, husband, and kids. On the other hand, I wanted to make a difference in the world by creating positive change.

When I finally allowed myself to reflect on my mom's passing, however, I realized that, despite our very real differences, I would always be my mother's child. As I took the time to understand her ways and what she stood for in life, I realized, in fact, that many of her ways were part of me—invisible to me at times, but right there beneath the surface of my existence. Given the right set of circumstances, my mother's ways surfaced and we became closer than we'd ever been while she was alive. Why? Because I had accepted the "she" in me.

After this period, my work took on another level of depth and clarity. I was willing to venture to the edges of chaos and confusion with clients and organizations in a way that I had not been capable of participating in the past. My sense of exploration deepened and my business solutions took on a new level of creativity and innovation. I had more energy to give and a higher level of curiosity that influenced not only my consulting process but my leadership ability as well.

I reclaimed something that I know to be true—that to broaden one's perspective and not judge others enhances one's ability to be effective. When we place judgment, we close the door to understanding and open the door to unconscious bias. We set up a dynamic that provides a preference on how we are going to or "should" operate. We don't allow for a natural interaction to emerge because our predisposition to a person or situation informs how we're going to react. We create a single narrative and allow that to guide our thoughts and processes.

Reflecting on and coming to acceptance of my mother—her leadership skills and her life model—provided me the emotional maturity to lead people far senior than I and to stand in my own center of confidence and wisdom. It was no longer about making someone or something wrong. Now, my focus and journey were about the partnerships that led to the right answers for that client, that organization, that leader.

People bring their whole selves to work—the good and the bad. Most of us experience life as fragmented experiences. We have to take the time to stop, reflect, and reconcile those experiences in order to grow from them.

Remember my friend Kim? Her reconciliation with her father came partly through the intervention of her husband. During a visit from her father, Kim's husband recognized the pain her dad's presence created and he finally decided to do something about it. Kim was 38—it had been

22 years since her parents' divorce—and her husband believed it was time to heal those wounds.

"I don't understand why you haven't talked about the issue," he said to his father-in-law. "It causes her pain and you pain."

They had tried a few times to reconcile, but, as the saying goes, the words got in the way. This time they were ready. They stayed up all night talking through their pain.

"He had, genuinely, blanked it all out," Kim said. "While I remember verbatim what was said, it wasn't until I told him that he remembered. After 22 years the truth came out as seen from both sides."

The relationship isn't perfect, but it's improving. Kim's father is more accommodating, and she's learned to forgive him. She's a very serious person, but she's been able to release the energy she was holding onto around her pain and put that energy into her own family and professional life.

"My lesson as a leader is that you are a sum total of your experiences," Kim told me.

> You are shaped by those moments and by people who helped you along the way. Your values, your beliefs, your triggers, all of it have influenced how you show up today, how you manage and how you lead. While I believe I reconciled it within myself a long time ago, actually talking to him objectively made it all dissolve even more. I saw him for what he was—just another human being trying to sort out his past. He wasn't angry, he didn't excuse things; he simply listened and then apologized. I was in awe.

Reconciliation is a big part of reflection. It's not the next step; it's an extension. It involves taking the self-discovery, including the failures, and making peace with them. Once we've reconciled our past, it's easier to become transparent about it. We move from the old—"My past defined me"—to the new—"My past is part of my life story." We eliminate the "poor me" attitude that's self-destructive and unappealing. We achieve the harmony, compatibility, consistency, and agreement that define reconciliation.

The Retrospective View

Understanding our crucible experiences through reflection leads to reconciliation. And that creates a self-awareness that lets us tap into talents we didn't know we had. It also allows us to live with a sense of peace and freedom.

We understand, like Mallik Angalakudati, the sources behind our driven nature, so we can tap into that work ethic but also learn to balance it against the need to spend time with family. We learn, like Kim, how to self-manage our serious nature. We learn how to embrace the gifts handed to us from others. In my case, they were gifts from my mother.

When we reconcile things within ourselves, we also learn to deal with disappointments and setbacks, those of our creation and those that are beyond our control. If we've done as much as we can do, we can leave it there and move on—with the right attitude.

For instance, if we get passed over for a promotion in favor of someone less qualified, we're faced with some choices about how to react. We can stay and choose to understand why we didn't get the promotion, thus developing as a professional, or we can leave. Either way, we can use the experience as motivation or it can become a source of anger and bitterness. We can harbor resentment, there or at our next job. We can make excuses about our failings and erect a wall around us with no doors or windows for advancement. Or we can reflect on it as a crucible experience, learning from the realities it exposed and determining to move forward because of who we are rather than staying stuck in who we are.

The latter choice allows for a greater reservoir of possibilities as we make decisions as a manager or as we manage others who are going through a cycle where they may be experiencing the untapped talent syndrome.

Learning from crucible experiences teaches us (and those we lead) something about ourselves that connects us to a higher purpose—something in our lives that's greater than ourselves and our personal goals. That purpose releases us from the bondage of circumstances, because we're focused on something bigger and more important than whatever we might find inconvenient or difficult in the moment. Very often, we learn that another, far better door has opened as the one we thought we wanted to walk through was closing. When we are focused on a higher purpose, what's right for us will manifest, even if it feels wrong or difficult in the moment. Sometimes what's right is what's most difficult. We often think what's right for us is the smooth, easy road. But there's something in the context of the difficult that's needed to get us to what's next. That's the value of the crucible experience, but we have to identify it, reflect on it, and reconcile it. Otherwise, it becomes another link in our chain's mediocrity—or, worse, the chains that imprison us.

Let me give you an extreme example of the type of crucible experience that defines a person—for better or for worse.

Recently, I read a story about a young man whose behaviors in middle school were so disruptive that the school's administrators finally suspended him for a week. He returned and the disruptive behavior continued. He was rude, aggressive, and filled with rage. Again he was suspended. Eventually, the boy's teacher, accompanied by a police officer, went to his home, where they interrupted the boy's mother in her work as a prostitute. It turned out that the boy behaved badly so the school would send him home because his mom wouldn't "work" when he was home and he didn't want her working.

"The boy never hated school, he just loved his mom more," said Cord Jefferson, a writer whose mother was the boy's teacher.

A young man like that isn't without talents. Indeed, compassion and loyalty spring to mind immediately. But would those talents, and others he might possess, ever get tapped in a work setting? Would his managers see these talents in him? Would he see them in himself?

The answer depends largely upon how the young man reconciled his crucible experience. I don't know what happened to the boy, but I do know that part of his experiences shaped him in multiple ways, and most of them could play out in his career. With reflection and reconciliation, he might tap into the compassion and loyalty he showed for his mother. He might become a great leader. Or, his antisocial behavior might become the norm and rage might define him. His untapped talents would stay untapped.

The sooner we take a retrospective view of our lives, the sooner we develop the path to something better. If we can look back with humility, honesty, and discernment, we can create a plan for change. That's not easy, but that's what we have to do if we want to experience what life can really offer.

When you're "in it," all your senses are razor-focused on the specific situation—the unfairness of it, the pain of it, the challenges of it. When you move out of it and create a new normal, then you have an opportunity to look back with perspective.

We all have crucible experiences, and the sooner we reflect on them and reconcile with them, the sooner we can embrace a discovery process that exposes our untapped talents. You can take any number of assessments to figure out the things you're good at, but the deeper, more valuable things about who you are and what you have to offer won't truly emerge until you explore your life and connect it to a higher purpose.

When you've done that, you're not only improving your ability to fully tap into your own talents, but you're also uniquely positioned to identify the untapped talent around you and to help others develop the personal soundness that will change their lives.

LEADERSHIP EXERCISE: CRUCIBLE EXPERIENCES

When instructed to consider life experiences that have had a major impact, most people take some time to come up with several examples that have helped shaped their lives. Take your time with this process. Reflecting on the past is not always easy, but it leads to a better understanding of who you are and how your life has been influenced. It can also pinpoint strengths to use and challenges that need addressing in both your personal and professional lives.

1. Block an hour once a week for one month to reflect on your crucible experiences. They can be business or personal incidents.
2. Sketch pictures that represent those experiences, then write a paragraph on each experience and how they may connect to your current professional experience. Don't judge what emerges during your discovery process. Let the story unfold naturally so you don't miss the critical turning points. Sometimes there are small junctures that appear unimportant but, when integrated, have a major impact.
3. Share your story with at least two trusted friends. Get their feedback on what lessons you can learn from them and how your story aligns with their experience of you. How we see ourselves and how others see us is critical in understanding our strengths and untapped talent. We may display behaviors unconsciously that block our success or are such a strong part of our DNA, they contribute to our success without us knowing or realizing why.
4. Reach out to others, if necessary, to reconcile personal or professional wounds. This is always a cathartic experience, if the other person wants to participate. Sometimes reconciliation is not about others but about you coming to terms with a situation. It can be that simple and that complicated.
5. Identify ways you can and will live differently in light of this exercise. This is where you treat yourself to a new existence. Imagine "big," go for all it's worth. The good news is you can always scale back if reality dictates.

PART III
Exemplifying

This page intentionally left blank

CHAPTER 8

The Three Rs: Emerging from the Hidden Workforce

This page intentionally left blank

This world is clearly emerging before our eyes. The shifts ahead, the opportunities ahead are massive.
—Carly Fiorina, business executive

Mining the untapped talent in the hidden workforce can yield higher productivity, new answers to old problems, more effective teams, a culture of talent stewardship...In short, it produces leaders with the capacity to create better results.

The need for strong, capable leaders is greater than ever. Our world is changing at a speed unknown to previous generations, and it's critical to organizational success to have people in key position who know how to lead and manage in our diverse, dynamic, speed-driven society.

Bob Johansen, a distinguished fellow at the Institute for the Future, believes many leaders today are overwhelmed with a world full of volatility, uncertainty, complexity, and ambiguity. In *Leaders Make the Future*,[1] the book Johansen authored in 2012, he suggests that leaders' decision-making efforts are impacted by their inability to process in today's chaotic world. Future leaders, he says, need a new set of skills and principles. His leadership principles deal with the ability to anticipate, to stay healthy physically and mentally, to filter out noise and distractions, to know and challenge, to share stories that help people imagine a future, and to act with courage and clear intent in an authentic, engaging, and self-effacing way.

I wholeheartedly agree with Johansen's contention that those skills are needed in today's leaders, except for one point. We already have leaders in today's work environment who are very good at living and working in chaos, managing ambiguity, and dealing with the unknown. They can be found in the hidden workforce. We just have to discover the leader within the hidden workforce.

Leaders who are stuck in the hidden workforce typically exemplify three primary characteristics that provide them a competitive advantage in today's business world: resourcefulness, resilience, and resolve—human characteristics of leadership that too often are overlooked and underdeveloped. With a little help, we can lead this significant group of employees to be successful managers and leaders who contribute to our organization's success.

There's a long list of skills and traits that are common among people who succeed in life and in work, and you've likely seen them and read about most of them: Integrity, hard work, vision, problem-solving, humility, intelligence, ambition, and on and on the list goes. Authors like Bob Johansen added to it regularly, sometimes with legitimately new skills and sometimes with updated versions on the old skills.

We've already discussed some of those characteristics and soft skills, and we'll go into more as we move along. But this section focuses on resourcefulness, resilience, and resolve, because they represent something critical in the discussion of untapped talent.

These characteristics are the building blocks of great leadership and they're at the core of every great leader you'll ever encounter. They are interwoven into all the other leadership skills you'll ever find, including the "new" ones presented by Johansen and others. They are timeless and essential. And, most important, they are prominently present, although often hidden, in the lives of people whose talents typically go untapped.

People who come to success through nontraditional pathways have no other choice but to maximize their resources, rely on resilience, and display their resolve when presented with roadblock after roadblock. Many start off with minimal resources; they come from backgrounds where abundance was measured by family relationships, personal beliefs, and the will to be successful—all extremely important characteristics that helped shaped who they became. Through their perseverance, they learned how to anticipate, how to remain focused, how to tackle challenges, and certainly how to be authentic. They embody resourcefulness, resilience, and resolve.

When they are identified and developed as leaders—when their talents are tapped—they emerge from the hidden workforce and become great, not just good, leaders.

In fact, my experience working with companies and top leaders across the world tells me that resourcefulness, resilience, and resolve are the common threads among the talent and leaders that emerge from the hidden workforce. If you studied their lives and careers, as I have, you'll see that those characteristics were at the root of their ultimate success.

Most people with untapped talent—those who aren't funneled into the talent pipelines because they lack the traditional markings of a high-potential leader—already have resourcefulness, resilience, and resolve. But many of them don't realize they have those qualities, because they've never stopped to consider it and because those qualities were nurtured in informal ways, sometimes outside of their work environments. And it becomes a leader's job to find it right under their noses.

Those qualities were a huge part of the reason they advanced to a certain level, but they often go unrecognized by either the person who has them or by that person's supervisors. They can become the invisible characteristics of people in the hidden workforce.

We're going to unpack those characteristics and see what they are, how they differ from each other, how to identify them in others (and in yourself), how to develop them, and how to make the most of them. We'll do that partly by looking at how they played a key role in the lives of successful leaders who emerged from the hidden workforce because those key characteristics didn't go untapped.

You'll see resourcefulness in Zaid Abdul-Aleem. He grew up on the Southside of Chicago, where his mother worked three jobs at times to keep him and his sister in private schools. From an early age, Zaid learned how to make the most of the resources around him—starting with his family—and that resourcefulness has taken him around the world and to a top position in the financial services industry.

You'll see resilience in the story of Anne Smithson. Anne's teen years were tumultuous, to say the least, but she emerged from her troubled youth and eventually worked her way through college. Now she's an executive at a Fortune 100 company.

And you'll see resolve in Denise Draper. Denise came to the United States from Puerto Rico with high expectations, but faced roadblocks along the way that tested and developed her resolve. The biggest test came when she found herself in a new high-level job in an industry she was still learning with a disgruntled ex-coworker at a competing company actively working to bring her down.

As a leader in an organization who might have some untapped talents, resourcefulness, resilience, and resolve are three characteristics you can identify within your background and tap into as you emerge into newfound roles and responsibilities. Seeing them in yourself can help you gain the self-confidence to face the inevitable challenges that come with realizing your potential in life.

And as a leader who is responsible for talent management—those of you who want to create a culture of talent stewardship and who want to identify, nurture, and advance talent that all too typically goes untapped—you can home in on these characteristics in the people around you.

Resourcefulness, resilience, and resolve are strong characteristics you want in the people you nurture and promote within your organization, but their influence on untapped talent is even broader than that. Understanding the stories behind the resourcefulness, resilience, and resolve that you see in the hidden workforce will help you see all sorts of other skills that are born of those traits.

It will help you connect the dots between people's experiences and their potential to apply what they've learned in new settings so that they can make the most of their careers. That might mean you've spotted the corporation's next CEO, or it might mean you've found someone who can move from an individual contributor to a team leader. Or from a team leader to a manager. Or from a manager to a director. Or from a director to a vice president. There are endless possibilities.

Emerging from the hidden workforce isn't about getting on the fast track to the executive suites. Indeed, not everyone is going to be a chief executive officer, an executive vice president, a senior vice president, a city manager, or, in government-speak, a "Super Grade 17." Nor does it make sense to have a world full of c-suite leaders. Tasks and responsibilities need to be dissected and assigned to those with the skills who can best accomplish the tasks. Strategic thinkers usually aren't proficient at tactical assignments.

We all have a talent ceiling based on our skills, abilities, exposures, intellect, dedication, and discipline to practice our crafts. And we all have differing ambitions. Some people totally accept their positions in the hierarchy of productivity. They reach a point at which the time and effort it would take to increase their productivity simply isn't worth the price they'd pay in lost time for spending with family, friends, hobbies, and other outside work interests. They are likely tapping into most of their talents, but putting self-imposed limits on their work lives.

For the people on your teams, emerging from the hidden workforce is about recognizing their untapped talents and putting them to use. This is a key step to finding contentment in work and in life—and to advancing their careers. And no matter what that looks like for each one individually, it's sure to include resourcefulness, resilience, and resolve.

This page intentionally left blank

CHAPTER 9

Seeing Solutions: The Role of Resourcefulness

This page intentionally left blank

We learn the ropes of life by untying its knots.
                              —Jean Toomer, poet and novelist

A friend of mine was vacationing with family in North Carolina when several of them decided to take a sailing outing. The plan was simple. They would charter a sailboat and make a round trip up and down the sound between the Outer Banks and the inland coast.

The motley crew boarded the boat and followed the orders of Captain Peggy, who instructed them on various tasks as they moved out of the harbor. As they prepared to hoist the sails, she asked one of the guys to turn the helm to the right and hold it. He turned and turned and turned, applying pressure on it as he awaited instructions from Captain Peggy to do something different. He put so much pressure on it, however, that the cable from the helm to the rudder snapped. No working rudder equals no steering. The boat floundered in the middle of the shipping channel as Captain Peggy weighed her options.

First, she radioed her base and reported the problem.

"OK," her boss said.

Next she watched as another boat came out and moved toward them. And then she watched as that boat raised its sail and cruised by with its own passengers.

Confused, Captain Peggy radioed her base again.

Here's the gist of what she was told: Figure it out.

So Captain Peggy began rigging a manual steering mechanism to work the rudder, and ten minutes later she and her passengers were sailing across the sound.

Captain Peggy employed a simple formula you might have seen before:

Necessity + Creativity + Persistence = Resourcefulness.

As a leader, resourcefulness isn't an optional characteristic—for you or for your organization. It's essential. Why? Because we live and lead in complex times that are filled with unexpected twists and turns, not to mention the occasional broken rudder cable. The nature of "work" now involves multiple moving and interconnected parts that change often, and those changes send ripples from city to city, from culture to culture, and from one industry to another. A business decision made in Toledo at an auto parts plant can affect the business strategy of the software developer in India, which can alter the tactics of the cosmetics manufacturer in South America.

When changes and chaos come—*when*, not *if*—the leaders who adapt are the leaders who survive, and resourcefulness is the key to adapting in the midst of chaos and change.

Paul Graham, a software pioneer who, among other things, now provides financial and hands-on support to startups, wrote a blog in 2009 in which he said he had finally boiled down what it takes to be a "good startup founder" to just two words: "relentlessly resourceful."[1]

I like that phrase, but I think Graham uses it too narrowly. To him, it fits primarily for founders of startups, and not so much for the rest of us.

"This isn't the recipe for success in writing or painting, for example," Graham wrote. "In that kind of work the recipe is more to be actively curious. Resourceful implies the obstacles are external, which they generally are in startups. But in writing and painting they're mostly internal; the obstacle is your own obtuseness."

In my experience, resourceful doesn't imply that obstacles are external. Whether your obstacles are internal or external, they're still stopping you from moving forward, and you need to "figure it out" so you can get moving again. So I'd argue that every leader needs resourcefulness. If an organization's resourcefulness stops with its founder, the organization will flounder. Indeed, that's why too many startups don't become "stay ups."

Curiosity, by the way, is simply a piece of the resourcefulness puzzle. If you want to be resourceful, ask a lot of questions, look at things from a fresh perspective, learn something new every chance you get, do things differently. Live curiously. And that curiosity will inspire and support your resourcefulness.

As a leader, resourcefulness is a critical characteristic to develop in yourself and in the talent around you. The potential of untapped talent remains limited when they aren't displaying resourcefulness. Rather than acting on their resources, they're acting on their limitations. Instead of having their heads and hands open and outstretched, they are only bartering on their own mindset and knowledge. Sometimes they fail to see the unlimited possibilities right in front of them.

On the other hand, we know from experience that resourceful people get things done. They are the ones we turn to when there's a challenge and a tight deadline. They have a knack for "figuring it out." And as leaders working on tight time and financial budgets, we love people with a knack for figuring things out.

As leaders and managers, however, we tend to lean on the same group of superstars and avoid the important task of developing or discovering resourcefulness in the people around us who don't always display it in the obvious ways. Thus, we end up leading from our limitations, not our resources.

For untapped talent, resourcefulness often lies dormant or, at best, surfaces only on rare occasions because it's not utilized. They are resourceful in certain settings, but not always at work. So they might show tremendous resourcefulness while volunteering at a nonprofit organization or helping out with their church or mentoring a student, but they don't show that same resourcefulness in their jobs. Or they showed great resourcefulness in extreme circumstances—as a serviceperson during war or responding during a disaster, for instance—but never apply those skills in their work. Or they displayed resourcefulness in their educational journeys or early in their work careers as they rose to a certain level, but then they hit roadblocks—some of their own making and others made by circumstances or other people. So they slipped into the status quo, where resourcefulness gets choked to near death.

For untapped talent to emerge from the hidden workforce, it must free itself from the status quo. It must tap into its resourcefulness. So the challenge for leaders is to spot the Captain Peggys who are hiding among them and develop them into the leaders who can bring meaningful results to their organization.

Day-to-Day Resourcefulness

Resourcefulness operates in the day to day because not a day goes by when some sort of resourcefulness isn't needed to advance a task, a project, or a strategy—to solve some problem that's sprung up. If you and your teams don't encounter problems or challenges at work, then you need new work that challenges you.

But, of course, you and your team have challenges—every day. And you have people who simply aren't rising to those challenges. So you have to develop your resourcefulness and the resourcefulness in the people around you.

Resourcefulness is simply identifying the resources available to you and putting them to the best use to achieve your goals. It doesn't matter whether the goal is a simple task or a complex challenge, nor does it matter if the challenges are external or internal.

When we think about "resources," we naturally focus on the tangible—things like materials or money. We can't build a cathedral without bricks, right? And we can't build a marketing program without a budget, right? But two resources are even more foundational, especially to untapped talent: yourself and your networks.

Untapped talent unlocks their resourcefulness when they learn to manage their "self" (their internal resources) and their networks (their external resources). That's how they can get the bricks and the budget and the other physical resources they need.

Tapping into Resourcefulness

Resourcefulness can seem like a gift that many of us never received—an innate talent that came from the hand of God, like Michael Jordan's competitiveness or Luciano Pavarotti's passion. That's great for the chosen few, but it doesn't help those who are trying to tap into their talents and it doesn't help leaders who are trying to find and develop that resourcefulness in the untapped talent on their teams.

Yes, resourcefulness is something of an innate ability. You and your team might never achieve extreme levels of resourcefulness any more than you could develop Michael Jordan's level of competitiveness or Luciano Pavarotti's level of passion.

On the other hand, maybe you can. If not, you certainly can improve. I know this because I've also learned that there are processes for tapping into resourcefulness that allow it to flourish in anyone. And, in fact, untapped talent generally originates from backgrounds and experiences that uniquely equip them with skills and abilities. They end up untapped talent because they are different from the norm, but they've survived those differences enough to achieve some successes in life.

Resourcefulness is there; in other words, it's just untapped.

So let's look at some ways you can tap into your team's talent in a more powerful way. These aren't in sequential order; they are processes that can build on each other and that often need to happen simultaneously. They all help build the "self" and the "networks" that produce resourcefulness in untapped talent.

Tapping into Yourself

The most critical and the obvious place to start mining your resources is within yourself—your intellect, your skills, your spiritual resources, and your experiences—and approaching life and work with confidence.

You might not think of self-confidence as a "resource," but it's the key ingredient that allows people to step into the unknown and face something when there's no roadmap, no proven way to deal with it. Doing that requires self-confidence—an unshakeable belief that, yes, you can figure it out.

Here are some ways to grow the confidence in the untapped talent around you:

Emphasize the investment. One of the first things you need to help people change and grow is buy-in from your team. They might not voice it out loud, but they'll ask the question: "What's in it for me?" You need to have an answer, and it needs to include this: "I believe in you, so I'm investing in you." If you tell them—and, more importantly, show them—that you believe they are important to the organization and, more importantly, to you, then you'll get a good return on your investment. If they don't believe they are a good investment, they'll never work with full confidence in themselves.

Teach them the rules. Put them in environments that teach them the stated and unstated rules of your organization's culture. Information breeds self-confidence, and half the battle is simply learning the rules of the game. Untapped talent, however, often comes from backgrounds that are played by rules different from the rules of society at large or the business culture.

The sooner they internalize the unwritten and often unspoken rules of the culture, the more confidently they'll approach their work.

Challenge them to face their fears and face the consequences. Stepping into the unknown typically comes with that uneasy heart-in-the-throat feeling. Untapped talent often needs encouragement to take the leap of faith that inevitably comes with occasional failure. They need to know they will have to face the consequences, but that you and other leaders will support them through that process.

Connect their dots. Untapped talent lives in the trenches, but sometimes they need someone to help them see the view from thirty thousand feet. For starters, they need to see that their nonwork resourcefulness applies to work-life challenges. Lessons in resourcefulness they learned in their family, in their neighborhood, in their school, in their community—all translate into lessons they can apply at work. Next, remind them of their wins at work, because they can lean on those victories when they're facing a new challenge. Finally, help them take a long-term view, which minimizes the impact of setbacks. Resourcefulness is about taking risks, and a long-term view helps you get back up when the risks don't work out. It builds resilience and confidence.

Tapping into Your Networks

Help from others should begin with those who are closest to them—their managers and mentors, for starters. As a leader in an organization, it's your responsibility to grow the talent around you, and one way you do that is by helping employees connect to the external resources they need to display resourcefulness.

Here are some ways to do that:

Open the access. As discussed earlier in chapter two access is one of the things most lacking in the professional lives of untapped talent. Access is a resource. I heard a story recently about a woman who was opening an orphanage in Africa. She had the land, the buildings, the workers, and, of course, the children—64 of them. What did she lack? Water. And the problem wasn't a lack of water; the problem was she lacked access to the water. In her case, access would cost $15,000. With no water, there would be no orphanage.

Untapped talent typically lacks access to a well with a different type of resource—key people. They often don't share the cultural connections to higher-level leaders, so they don't run in the same circles. As a leader, you can help by connecting them to people of influence and by getting those key leaders to invest in your people. Seek others' opinions and listen to their advice, then ask them to commit to helping the people around you achieve their goals. That commitment can look like words of encouragement, but it also can take more formal forms like mentoring or giving your people stretch assignment or cross-departmental tasks.

In the same way, you need to encourage those around you to identify and mine their networks. These are the people they already know or can connect with through people they already know. It might be a pastor or a friend from college or someone they've met through a professional networking organization.

Grow their expertise. Resourcefulness doesn't come without knowledge. It involves risks, of course, but those risks are informed by experience and by formal education. Encourage and support employees to take part in appropriate business and leadership training, to volunteer for stretch assignments, to volunteer in their community, and to read great books and articles. This extends their networks to anyone who's ever written a book, delivered a webcast, or taught a class.

Don't limit them to things related to their current job assignment. Help stretch them to become experts in anything that interests them, including work in fields that are different from their own. Help them cast a broad net. Maybe they've always wanted to learn to act or play the trumpet or take cooking lessons or improve their math skills or learn another language.

The more they learn, the more they have to offer, and the better they become at evaluating the strengths and weaknesses of a situation so they can pinpoint their opportunities. Then they can create informed strategies and go to work with a dedicated focus.

This produces the side benefit of helping build their self-confidence.

The Face of Resourcefulness

I've worked with dozens of men and women who've found themselves stuck in the hidden workforce. When I look at what they need in order to break free, I always connect the dots back to the people I know who have "figured it out." Those people—many of whom where untapped talent at some stage or stages of their careers—all discovered how to tap into their resourcefulness.

Zaid Abdul-Aleem, a bright young executive in the financial services industry, discovered this early in life. The things he learned from his family, teachers, mentors, and through self-study helped him develop a resourcefulness that has taken him from humble beginnings on the Southside of Chicago to college at Duke University to personal and professional success all around the world.

He is a man with a history of making the most of the resources around him to achieve success in life, which is why he emerged early from the hidden workforce.

Is his resourcefulness innate or developed? The answer is "both."

As a child, Zaid was supported by a strong mother and extended family that helped him look at the successful people around him and then at his own successes, and he used those early experiences to polish his self-confidence in his resourcefulness. Each achievement, especially those that bucked the odds, became a confidence builder for the next, even more unlikely accomplishment. His success stories became the stepping stones for his life.

Zaid learned early that it took time for big projects to succeed, which helped him develop patience and a strong work ethic as success played out. He learned how to take a long-term view.

"If you have a goal and you have work ethic and you have discipline and you align yourself in a positive way to something that really resonates with you, then it's going to be realized," he told me. "It really is about discipline, work ethic, and staying focused on the objective."

What happens when you run into an obstacle? Resilience and resolve play their part, but here's where resourcefulness comes in: Resourceful people act with confidence, create informed strategies, and go to work with a dedicated focus.

For many people, especially those who've slipped into the trap of the hidden workforce, distractions are the death of resourcefulness. They get distracted because they are focused on their failures and things that have kept them from succeeding in the past. "Why not?" becomes "why bother?"

Zaid faced a crossroad when his mother enrolled him in a private school. His family didn't have much money, so she was working two and sometimes three jobs to pay his tuition. His classmates, meanwhile, came mostly from wealthy families, practiced different religions, and looked very different from him. When he faced challenges and setbacks, however, he didn't let his background or his skin color or his family's lack of financial wealth become a distraction that slowed him down.

"When I went to schools where most people didn't look like me, I was very comfortable with who I was," he said.

> If I wasn't excelling like they were, it was just a matter of how I could gain confidence in that area. I didn't personalize it or internalize it based on me being different from them... As long as it's not personal, something I can't control like the color of my skin, then it's just a matter of figuring it out.

Lots of factors can become distractions to that type of focus: Office politics, opportunity, being marginalized, institutional racism, personal insecurities... But the people who overcome those barriers are the ones who build the confidence that takes them out of the hidden workforce.

Zaid's self-confidence grew with his success and he began to expand his networks. Thanks to his mother's influence, Zaid was exposed to a good formal education that included extracurricular activities such as sports, music, and art. But he also began networking with people, turning them into resources to help him achieve his goals.

As a teenager, Zaid approached business leaders in Chicago and asked them to invest in him by paying his way to Paris between his junior and senior years of high school at Lake Forest Academy. Why? He wanted to improve his ability to speak French.

This part of Zaid's story is a good general example of resourcefulness at work, as well as a specific example of the importance of using networks. First, Zaid recognized that he had a problem: He didn't speak French as well as his classmates. Second, he wasn't satisfied with his "average" grades, and he was self-motivated to get better. Third, he figured out the reasons for his problem: Most of his peers had spent time in France and he had never been there. Fourth, he didn't make excuses or give up simply because there was no easy fix to his dilemma. Instead, he came up with a solution: Go to France. And then he came up with a plan for reaching that goal.

For most people in Zaid's situation, Paris would have become one of two things: A long-range goal or a quickly forgotten dream. But Zaid had the will to find a way.

He began by putting together a list of prominent CEOs. Some were relatives or friends of his classmates; others were donors to the school whose names he got from the headmaster. Then he wrote letters asking those leaders to send him to Paris for the summer—not on a vacation and not as an act of charity, but as an investment.

"I wrote a letter saying I was a student-athlete, president of my class, captain of my team, blah, blah, blah, and that I felt I deserved to go to Paris to improve my academic skills and grades," Zaid said. "And if you invest in me, I told them, I guarantee a good return on your investment."

Tom Dittmer, the cofounder of the legendary commodities trading company Refco Inc., lived in Lake Forest and found himself intrigued by Zaid's request. He invited Zaid to his home to learn more about him. Dittmer recognized a good investment when he saw it, and he probably saw a little of himself in the young Zaid. Dittmer wasn't born into wealth, and many of his breaks came from creatively taking advantage of the resources around him. So he agreed to send Zaid to Paris. He took care of Zaid's housing and got him a summer job working at the Paris stock exchange.

When Dittmer funded Zaid's summer experience in Paris, Zaid learned more than how to improve his French or how the stock exchange operates. He also learned the value of networks—including his place in the networks of other people. He learned that when others helped him, he provided value back to them—it wasn't a one-way street. And not only did he help them in practical, functional ways (e.g., he accomplished specific tasks), but he also helped them by becoming part of their legacies. Now he looks for others to join in his legacy.

"You have to appreciate people and what everyone has to offer and what you can learn from them," Zaid told me.

> It's recognizing that no person is an island. If I meet someone that I respect and I'm interested in them as a person and the things they do and say to me, then I see that person as someone I would want to keep a relationship with. Ultimately, I have a number of people in my life like that. I get fulfillment from the relationship, and it builds an enterprise. When I invite them together, there are synergies created from that.

Zaid can trace his resourcefulness back to the influence of his mother and other key figures in his childhood who proactively encouraged him and disciplined him and pushed him so that he had the tools and the confidence for success. The untapped talent in your organization needs the same encouragement, discipline, and pushing, and don't think they're too old to change. For most of them, the resourcefulness already is there. They will welcome the chance to display it.

LEADERSHIP EXERCISE: CHARTING RESOURCEFULNESS

Consider the resources you have available to you in your job. Are they adequate? How effectively are you using them, and are there ways to increase your effectiveness when applying your arsenal of techniques, tactics, and strategies?

To answer those questions, you must assess the current state of your resources and your ability to be resourceful. To help with this exercise, fill in the diagram here. It should provide a picture that translates the relationship between your internal and external resources.

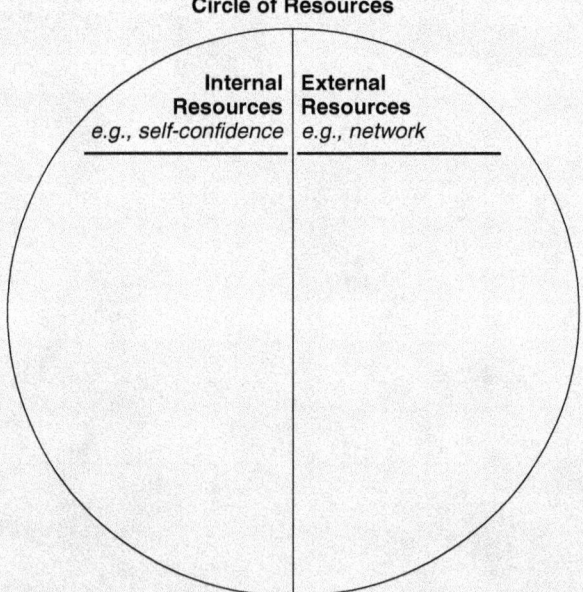

What key themes emerge from the diagram? Are there any surprises or reasons for concern? How can you reposition your resources to have greater impact?

For an in-depth analysis of your and your team's resourcefulness, you can take the extended survey on resilience, resourcefulness, and resolve by going to www.centerfocus.com.

CHAPTER 10

Failing Forward: The Role of Resilience

This page intentionally left blank

> Sometimes Grace comes in the form of a punch in the face.
> —Mary Elder

Anne Smithson is an executive in one of the largest corporations on the planet, and her journey includes several examples of resourcefulness and resolve. What stands out the most to me, however, is her incredible resilience—and the role her resilience played in moving her out of the hidden workforce.

So, what do I mean by resilience?

When I think of resilience, I think about the ability to bounce back well from the difficult things life hands us. For Anne, whose real name I'm not sharing out of respect for her privacy, life handed out homelessness, periods when she was ostracized by her own family, and a marriage and pregnancy at the age of 18.

Life, as we all know, can be difficult. People get hit by all sorts of adversity—illnesses, poverty, abuse, the death of loved ones, injustices, divorce, natural disasters...you name it. Resilience is the ability to pick yourself up after a traumatic situation and start again, or to redefine yourself when something has come to an end, or to adjust when you don't get what you wanted (or what you deserved). It's about bouncing back and, in fact, growing even stronger from the adversity, not giving into it and sinking into despair or depression.

In psychological terms, resilience is a process, not a trait. It develops from "confronting stressful experiences and coping with them effectively."[1]

It's the process of coping with stress and adversity. The trait is "resiliency." So split those hairs if you'd like, but here's what I've seen in leaders who tap into their talents: They successfully bounce back from adversity. They are resilient.

Resilience in the workplace is important to understand because, again, none of us are immune to troubles. There's an old saying: You're either in the middle of a trial, coming out of a trial, or about to enter a trial. If you worked long enough, you undoubtedly will face situations where one or more of your employees or coworkers are experiencing setbacks and challenges. How they respond to those challenges is partly a product of your ability to build their capacity for resilience. Most of us have never faced the challenges faced by Anne, but her story sheds some light on what resilience looks like and some insights into how we can spot it in others—or tap into it ourselves.

The Shaping of Anne

Anne was the middle child in a family raised by parents with strict religious beliefs. In early elementary school, Anne attended an international Muslim school in a large city. It was a melting pot of multinationals who shared the common bond of their religion. Some were US citizens, but others were natives of Africa or the Middle East.

That became Anne's normal.

In the second grade, however, her family moved, and she found herself in a different school with no one who looked like her.

"My first awareness of being very different was walking into my new second grade classroom, being the only black person, and having on a khimar," she said. "It wasn't until that moment that I realized I was different."

By the time she reached middle school, Anne had developed friends and found a fit among her classmates. She already was five feet, eleven inches tall (and on her way to six feet, two inches), and she was excelling on the school basketball teams.

Lesson 1. Anne teaches us that comfort may not be a lasting condition in our lives and that individual worldviews are not universally shared. Once we accept and learn how to adjust to people and situations around us, life can continue, perhaps not as we've known it, but as a new normal.

Anne's new reality brought challenges. In keeping with her religious beliefs, Anne kept her hair, arms, and legs covered when she played basketball. She didn't take part in secular holidays like Halloween or non-Muslim religious holidays like Christmas (although she once sang "White Christmas" at a school event without her parents' knowledge).

Anne adjusted. She figured out how to be herself—a tall girl and the middle child in a Sunni Muslim family—and still express herself as a singer, an athlete, a school leader, and a friend to kids she liked but who were in many ways very different from her and her family.

Lesson 2. Flexibility and accepting one's surrounding environment can bring a level of certainty that provides for growth, even if not all things in our life are as we would like them.

Then a series of events began reshaping Anne's world. It started when fire destroyed her family's house.

"The Red Cross put us up in a suite—two hotel rooms," she said. "And I remember my best friend's grandmother knocked on the door. She was Seventh Day Adventist. And she said, 'We knew you didn't have a stove, so we made dinner for your family.' The whole town took up a collection for my family, and everyone from every walk of life and every race gave to help us."

After the fire, Anne's family moved to a new community, and this time she had a much more difficult time adjusting. She was in another new school, starting over in a world where everyone already had their groups of friends. She still had her friends, too—they were just in a different town, attending a different school.

"When I was almost sixteen, I started talking on the phone to this guy," Anne said. "One of our first meetings was a disaster. I went to see him at his house without telling my parents. He lived in my old neighborhood, so it was a bus-ride away. When I got ready to go home, the bus didn't come and I was stuck."

Anne went to a friend's house to spend the night, but she called her parents the next morning to let them know she was okay.

"My parents thought I was ruined," she said. "I wasn't. But they basically said, 'We don't think you want to be a Muslim.' That's the first time I stopped covering my hair. My mom snatched my veil off my head."

Anne was told by her parents that she no longer could live with her family, that she had become a bad influence on her siblings, that they didn't think she accepted Islam, and that they were taking her to live with her aunt.

Things only got worse for Anne. She soon found herself hanging out with the wrong crowd, and she was sexually abused by several older men. Eventually, Anne's aunt decided she wasn't the solution to Anne's problems, and one night Anne awoke to find her mother had come for her. Her parents wanted to find a husband for her, thinking this was the only way to keep her life and reputation intact.

Anne, as you might imagine, wasn't a fan of this new plan.

"Something in me just said to run," Anne recalled. "And I ran. To this day, I just wish I had grabbed a bag of clothes."

Anne's aunt lived on the outer edges of the town, but a cab just happened to pass by. Anne flagged it down and took it to a friend's apartment. She beat on the door until someone answered, then borrowed some money to pay the fare. She had no money, no home, and no clothes other than the ones she was wearing. She no longer had a home, so she lived with whoever would let her stay the night.

Lesson 3. When difficult situations add stress to our lives, we may choose uncharacteristic solutions. We may seek comfort not in the familiar people who have assisted in our growth but in more foreign interactions that distract and take away from our positive life experiences.

But Anne didn't give in. Despite the stresses of her family and social life, for instance, Anne remained a good student.

"I was passionate about writing, and I was passionate about school," she said. "I was in honors classes. I went to school every day. I was in love with English class. There was never a question about going to school. It didn't occur to me until hindsight that it was hard. I would live wherever I could sleep, and I would find someone to drive me the five miles to school."

That lasted several months, but Anne eventually reconciled with her mother.

Lesson 4. Anne used her personal resources to stay anchored during this unnatural time. She tapped into something known as "emotional approach coping." It involves logical analysis, positive reappraisal of the situation, seeking guidance and support, and taking problem-solving actions. She believed school and her passion for English outweighed all that was happening. School and the joy it brought were what she needed to survive, and she found resources to help with that vision.

The next summer, after her junior year of high school, Anne met the man who would become her husband. She was 17 and he had just finished technical school with the Marines. At the insistence of Anne's father, the young man converted to Islam. Then he and Anne married a few months after she graduated from high school. A year after that, they had their first child.

"I was married and pregnant," she said. "All my friends were off in college, and I'm in a two-bedroom apartment in a college town working at a Wawa convenience store. I was a little devastated."

A large insurance company near her home was hiring temps from an agency to help with some clerical work, and Anne landed one of the jobs. It was the opening to her new beginning.

"I worked for a woman who became the communications department," Anne said. "I went in as a temp with the ability to write. She was a one-woman department. When they gave her a department, she asked me to be on her team. At the same time, I landed a full scholarship at the state university. I ended up going to work fulltime and going to school fulltime."

By the time she finished her undergraduate degree in English and communications, Anne had been promoted four times. She was leading a team of people who already had their degrees and who, as usual, looked very different from her and who had very different backgrounds from her.

"I'm always generationally different, racially different, gender different," she said. "But it's normal, because it's what I'm used to."

By anyone's standards, Anne's was successfully juggling the various parts of her life—a new husband, a new child, student responsibilities, and work demands. Anne was in the midst of creating a new life that was full of hope and possibility. Relying on her resilience skills to get her through all the multitasking and demands from various environments, she began to absorb her strengths and talents.

When Anne graduated from college, she left the insurance company. Despite the regular promotions, it was the one she didn't get that made her decide she needed a change.

"The woman who was my mentor was given another assignment in the company, and I thought I should have had her job," Anne said. "I was young but I helped build the department. I thought, 'How dare you not make me the manager?' They brought someone in who didn't like me. I knew I had to get out."

Lesson 5. Anne built on her successes. The more challenges she encountered and survived, the stronger she became—as a professional, a mother, and a person. Unconsciously, Anne was building on the resilience skills that were set in motion as a young girl changing schools for the very first time.

She continued to build her professional resume, changed jobs again after two years, and she moved up and up and up the corporate ladder.

When the corporation she was with went through a restructuring, she applied, on a whim, for a job as head of communications for Europe. Unexpectedly to her, she got it.

"I had never had a passport in my life until I took that job," she said.

The job wasn't a good fit, but Anne persevered. She reported to two men who came from caste-oriented cultures and who weren't used to having a woman on their team who spoke up as freely and forcefully as Anne did. And it didn't help that the job billed as "one-third travel" turned out to be "two-thirds" travel. Those travel demands did more than just keep her away from home; they brought additional cultural challenges.

"I learned I was American," she said with a laugh.

I didn't realize it. Traveling all over Europe, I learned I was not ready from a social perspective. My parents never had people over for dinner. I don't drink. I don't eat pork. Culturally, I wasn't socialized. I was not prepared at all to sit side-by-side with people who had a different upbringing. We had a guy come in and help me with my wardrobe. I had to learn how to dress, how to eat, how to not eat and do it discreetly, how to be conscious that when I talk I make big gestures.

Through it all, the experiences of her youth gave her confidence that she would figure things out and that she would bounce back successfully from each and every setback. And her background gave her some advantages that others lacked.

"I knew what it felt like to be in the minority, to always be different," she said.

I knew what it was like to have people impose and not listen. So in conversations traveling across Europe, people warmed up to me and listened, and I was able to listen and hear and bring people together from very disparate positions. As a middle child, I had experience trying to make peace. I knew about survival. I had developed the ability to connect disparate things.

Lesson 6. Anne learned that her early life experiences both supported her cross-cultural interactions and caused her stress. She built on her cultural competence skills in the areas she was deficient (learning to eat discreetly) and used her strengths and skills from being a minority to her advantage. She was, in fact, straddling a leadership dilemma that many of us face: the collusion of personal culture with organization culture and professional responsibility.

Anne now lives in the United States, where she works as an executive, runs her own international team, and reports directly to the president of a global division.

Building Resiliency

Global corporations are in need of people with the ability to bounce back, cope, reset their course of action, and renew their efforts. Business strategies that once changed every two years are now changing at an accelerated rate of every six months or quarterly depending on your revenue cycle. With more and more sophisticated ways of forecasting and tracking business, it's easy to determine what's working and what's not. This type of business environment requires quick, decisive actions with expedient methods for resolving outcomes. It also causes incredible stress, which leads to physical or mental conditions that impair leaders' effectiveness. In short, we need more leaders like Anne who are resilient and using their skills of managing through confusion and chaotic times while getting positive results.

What exactly should you be looking for in people who display strong resilience skills? Social scientists say you can see at least these four things in resilient people. One, they produce positive results even in high-risk situations. Two, they demonstrate competence even during the most stressful situations. Three, they recover quickly from traumatic situations. And, four, they grow from their failures and challenges, which allows them to more easily and quickly deal with future challenges. This last trait may be the one that is most useful in the work environment. Over time, resilient people begin to build a repertoire of successful projects and assignments, and their abilities to lead and be a strong performer increases.

As a manager, you have the ability to build the capacity for resilience in your team members. In a 2005 article in the *Journal of Leadership & Organizational Studies* titled "Leadership Behavior and Subordinate Resilience,"[2] the authors found a direct correlation between a leader's behavior and subordinate (their term) resilience, especially when transformational leadership characteristics were being demonstrated. By presenting a crisis as a challenge that can be resolved and with adequate support and guidance on the approach to problems, leaders can build their team members' resilience skills.

Being able to discern who is resilient on your team and who isn't provides you the opportunity to calibrate someone's development process. If you have a direct report who quietly avoids high-risk situations or who doesn't grow from mistakes or failures but instead blames others, you can help with growing his/her confidence. You may start with where they are on the emotional ladder of resilience and push the performance goal so it slightly pushes their comfort level. Once that comfort level is reached, you move the bar once again. Over time and with varying stimulators that add to their discomfort, they will slowly build their resilience skills.

Bob Bowman, the swim coach for Michael Phelps, used this technique to help Michael develop skills to deal with adversity during championship swim meets. He created training exercises unbeknownst to Michael that had him responding to organized, uncomfortable situations until Michael was capable of adjusting his emotional mode to address any inconsistencies in his performance environment. He even let Phelps race in a national junior meet without goggles. When Phelps forgot his goggles as he walked to the starting blocks, Bowman could have brought them to him. But he didn't. Phelps still won the race, and it proved a beneficial lesson in 2008 when Phelps's goggles filled with water as he swam the 200-meter butterfly in the Olympics. Phelps not only won that race, but did so in world-record time.

When you have direct reports who are resilient, it provides an opportunity to assign difficult and strategically important assignments to them.

You know they may falter, but they'll come out with a plan to manage the process to success. And they will overcome their frustrations and disappointment in a healthy way that moves work forward.

As a manager, your role is to provide the support for people to be successful. According to the American Psychological Association (APA), the primary factor in developing resilience is "having caring and supportive relationships within and outside the family. Relationships that create trust, provide role models, and offer encouragement and reassurance help bolster a person's resilience."[3]

The other most common factors, according to the APA, are the following:

1. The capacity to make realistic plans and take steps to carry them out.
2. A positive view of yourself and confidence in your strengths and abilities.
3. Skills in communication and problem solving.
4. The capacity to manage strong feelings and impulses.[4]

The untapped talent in today's business world often stays untapped not because it lacks resilience but because its resilience hasn't been put into play. It hasn't been spotted or developed, but it's very much like a muscle. It just needs to go to the gym.

Look for those around you who have experienced challenges in their lives and ask how their experiences have created a resilience that can help them thrive on your team and in a different stretch assignments. Put them to the test, and see if they don't bounce back stronger than ever.

LEADERSHIP EXERCISE: EVALUATING YOUR RESILIENCE

Think about a time in your career or life when you had a challenging situation and originally considered it insurmountable or it provoked undue anxiety.

1. Briefly describe the situation. What was happening? Who was involved? Over what period of time did this situation take place? How did you react?
2. How did you resolve it or what did you do to overcome the challenge?
3. What did you learn from this situation that you can apply in current challenges?
4. How much did the situation strengthen your ability to cope with challenges?
5. As a leader, what can you take from your experience and use it to improve your team's capacity for resilience?

For an in-depth analysis of your and your team's resilience capacity, you can take the extended survey on resilience, resourcefulness, and resolve by going to www.centerfocus.com.

CHAPTER 11

Standing Firm: The Role of Resolve

This page intentionally left blank

> Success is not final, failure is not fatal: It is the courage to continue that counts.
>
> —Winston Churchill

Denise Draper moved to the United States with all the hopes and dreams of any other smart, energetic young professional, but she learned pretty quickly that the marketplace was putting her in a box that would leave most of her talents untapped.

"I would say my first five years in the U.S. were very difficult," she told me. "I think people looked at my resume and it was hard for them to value my experiences."

Denise had a college degree and three years of work experience, but American employers typically saw her through a narrow lens. She was born and raised in Puerto Rico. She graduated from college in Puerto Rico. And all of her work experiences were in Puerto Rico. As one interviewer told her, "You've only worked with Hispanics."

Denise knew she had much more to offer than a lower-level role where her greatest contribution would be her ability to speak Spanish. So she began tapping into a leadership characteristic that she would develop and lean on for the rest of her life: Resolve.

"The fact that my first couple of years in the U.S. were difficult actually shaped me to understand that if I wanted to get where I wanted to get—if I wanted to reach my goals—I needed to get my MBA," she told me.

And that's what she did.

Denise drew on the resolve she learned as a child, largely from her parents and grandparents. It was a strong family unit that exemplified the payoff of resolve in very different ways. Her father was a civil engineer. Both of her grandmothers were college professors, and one of them also was an entrepreneur who, among other things, owned her own clothing store. Her mother, meanwhile, found contentment working part-time outside the home and fulltime as a homemaker. All of them showed her what resolve *looked* like, and those lessons paid off in her professional career.

They helped her push through graduate school while pregnant with her first child. They helped her juggle the demands of career and family as a single parent in the years that followed her divorce. They helped her move across diverse industries (from sales and marketing for consumer products to high-end financial services). And they allowed her to navigate some shark-infested waters when she took a top position in a bank only to find a key direct report had left for the competition and was taking several key staff members with him.

Denise overcame every unexpected twist, every unplanned turn, and every unpredicted setback in part because she developed and displayed resolve.

So when I picture "resolve," it looks a lot like Denise Draper.

Or Oscar Pistorius. Oscar ran the men's 400 meters at the 2012 Olympic Games in London. He didn't win a medal, but the South African did finish second in his quarterfinal heat with a time of 45.44 seconds. He also made it to the finals of the 4x400 relay as a member of the South African relay team. That's pretty darn good when you consider that he has no feet. Oscar, who had both legs amputated just below the knees at the age of 11 months, runs with two prosthetic legs. "I grew up not really thinking I had a disability," he said. "I grew up thinking I had different shoes."[1]

Like all Olympians, Oscar needed resolve to achieve his dream of competing in the Games, but his battles went beyond perseverance in training. First he had to convince the powers that be to allow him a chance to compete, because there were those who felt he had an unfair advantage in the two carbon fiber blades attached to the stumps of his legs. He applied and was rejected and appealed until he won the right to join the battle for a spot on that track at the Olympics. He failed to qualify for the 2008 Games by 0.7 seconds, but made it to London in the 400 meters and as a member of South Africa's relay team.

Resolve. That's Denise Draper. That's Oscar Pistorius. And that's the leadership characteristic you'll find in just about every successful leader you'll ever meet. That's why it's critical to identify and develop it in the untapped talent around you—because overcoming the obstacles that come with life takes time and, thus, an extended commitment to achieving our goals. It takes resolve.

Resourcefulness is all about making the most of the resources available to us, and resilience is all about bouncing back from the unexpected shifts that come our way. Resolve is about commitment. Indeed, it's about our commitment to our commitments. Resolve is that internal quality that drives our outward actions. It's the conviction that spawns ingenuity. It's the inner belief system that makes resilience possible. It's the burning desire and passion that fuels our focus and our discipline.

It's not just about not giving up, but also about simply getting up. Let's face it, work isn't always self-motivating. There are days when the elite athlete wants to sleep in rather than hit the pool or the track or the gym for another 6 A.M. workout. There are days when we show up and want to coast through the morning, maybe even the day, because we had a bad night or we had a great night or we experienced whatever external factor popped up to put us in a mood that suggested work could wait.

Resolve takes a stick and beats the lazy right out of procrastination; it gives us the same advice best-selling leadership author John Maxwell once got from his father: Pay now, play later.

It doesn't mean, however, we can't take a vacation or have fun; in fact, we can resolve to have a great time reaching whatever goals we might set—and then show resolve in achieving that goal.

Resolve begets resolve.

And that's what you have to pull out of the untapped talent—the resolve that's hidden within them, waiting to be tapped, waiting to be turned into more resolve that begets even more resolve.

As a manager, here are some things to keep in mind as you seek to untap the talent around you by providing opportunities and guidance for their resolve to develop.

Make Resolve Your Resolution

It's easy to identify the resolve in greatness. If you look at Olympians or titans of business or the champions in any endeavor, you'll see the part resolve played in their rise to the top. It's harder to see the potential for resolve in untapped talent. Make it a priority to seek it out and develop it.

In an earlier chapter, we talked a lot about spending time to get to know people beyond just their performance at work. The more you know about a person—personally as well as professionally—the better equipped you are to tap into that person's resolve. You'll get a feel for the person's passions, for how he or she handles success and failure, for when to push and when to back off.

A great leader, for instance, knows people well enough to notice when they can and should show greater resolve—when they are just sort of languishing and not pushing forward. They have a goal, but it's almost like they're avoiding the goal. They've gotten a project to a certain point, but they aren't moving it forward. Maybe they developed a fear of success that traps them in the status quo, or maybe they're just stuck on a problem and can't figure out the action planning steps they need to get them going again.

A friend of mine recently finished all of her course work for her doctorate from an Ivy League school, but she's putting off her dissertation. She's waffling around, coming up with all sorts of reasons (excuses) for not starting the project. In the meantime, it's becoming a big incompletion in her life.

Big incompletions block our energy and can spill over into other areas of our lives. We can develop a pattern of only getting so far on a project or assignment and then walking away or putting it aside because we simply can't see the next steps. We risk defining ourselves based on our incompletions, not on our successes. We don't develop the mental muscles and emotional stamina to move through the unknown. Our confidence takes a hit. And that sends us spiraling into the hidden workforce.

The better you know the people around you, the more likely you are to identify the trends in their lives that you can help them build on, as well as the trends you need to help them adjust to or eliminate from their lives.

Resolve is About Success...and Failure

When we look for resolve in the people around us, the tendency, as I said earlier, is too look for the successes in their lives. That's well and good, but the failures are just as important, if not more so.

Look for people who have grown from their disappointments, especially those who didn't handle an assignment the way they would have liked but then asked how they could do things differently the next time.

My first global training event involved multiple manufacturing groups from several different European countries. We were putting about 150 people through some challenging and emotionally revealing exercises. We worked with them in smaller groups of 20–30 people and, at times, as one large group. And as the event went on, we got more and more push-back about the exercises and their lack of relevance to the business. The chaos grew. The training wasn't effective. In short, my first big global event was unsuccessful to say the least.

So I asked myself a question: "What would I have done as a consultant that I didn't do for this event?" In retrospect, I realized I would have called all the business heads of all the countries and inquired about the state of the business, major changes, and any concerns they had that we should be aware of. We had relied on information from people with a limited understanding of the complexity of our work and its impact on the business; they knew plenty about the future plans specific to the manufacturing plants, but lacked the ability to translate those plans to the training teams. They knew that some of the plants were downsizing and that some, in fact, were expecting to close in the next year. The participants in the conference knew it, but we didn't. Thus the source of their angst! Had we known that plants were closing, we would have made some different decisions about training content and presentation. This became a major learning experience for us-how to work effectively with international organizations..

We also learned that all international work is local. Without understanding the local dynamics and accounting for their nuances, you'll inevitably experience limited success.

I grew from that disappointment and failure on how to deliver training internationally, and resolved that I was not going to repeat the experience. I was going to improve and do better the next time. And we—the team I worked with and I—showed a dramatic improvement with the next international event we led. Our evaluation scores increased 2.5 points or in the 90 percentile range! This pattern (our high scores) repeated itself throughout the course of work and world.

Untapped talent, of course, often fails to make that push without some help. As a leader, you need to challenge some people to do the self-evaluation that leads to self-improvement. You need to walk them through after-action reviews, asking questions such as, "How could you handle this differently next time?" and "What can I do differently next time to support your efforts?" As they see where they can improve and how it's possible to improve, they'll turn those disappointments into resolve.

Resolve Is About Pushing Hard... and Pushing Back

When we think of a person with resolve, we tend to focus on how hard he or she pushes toward a goal. And, indeed, it's common to find that untapped talent isn't pushing as hard as needed to achieve goals or learn from their disappointments. So sometimes you need to teach them to do more.

Then again, sometimes you need to show them when to do less.

A good leader understands his team's capacity for resolve, and uses that understanding to know when to elevate it and when to pull it back.

Why would you ever need to pull it back?

As a leader, a red flag should go up when you see someone whose resolve comes at the expense of taking care of himself or herself. Resolve becomes obsessive behavior, and the person can come off cranky, overly intense, short with coworkers, and, in many cases, physically ill. That makes the person less productive or even counterproductive. It might lead to some positive short-term results, but it typically leads to long-term disasters—burnout, cultural cancers, or a focus on some important skills at the expense of other important ones.

So your job isn't just to ignite resolve, but also lead with an awareness of when intensity isn't emotionally healthy for someone.

Resolve Revolves around Passion

The most effective way to build resolve in others is to tie it into the person's goals and something they feel passionate about. We're all motivated by our passions, so link as many operational goals as possible to the passions people already have.

Again, this ties back to really knowing the people who work around you—and what motivates them. If you don't know, you can't tie those passions to their goals.

Typically, this involves helping them see (and sometimes remember) the big vision of your organization or for their lives. Earlier in this chapter

I referenced the Olympics. That's a big-vision goal for any athlete, and it's the type of goal that fuels an athlete's resolve. It's what gets them up and going when they're worn out mentally and physically. With no vision—with no big goal—people's passions fade and they hit the snooze button on work.

The goals and the vision don't have to be about winning, they just have to be big enough to ignite someone's passion.

As leaders, we can provide the opportunities for people to define and reach their goals, plus guidance and support and resources they need to identify and pursue the things they are passionate about. When they own and tap into their passions, they'll tap into their resolve.

Resolve Is About the Process

Demonstrating resolve isn't always about the result; in fact, it's really much more about going through the process of doing the best you can do.

You don't always win the gold or the Super Bowl or get the big contract. So sometimes winning is about knowing that you worked as hard as you could and did the best that you could. So your commitment isn't to winning but to doing your best and striving toward the result. Results end up different for different people.

For some athletes, the goal is simply to get to the Olympic Games (Oscar Pistorius). For others, it's about winning the gold (Allyson Felix). For others, it's about winning multiple gold medals (Michael Phelps).

The Face of Resolve

When you invest in developing the resolve of the untapped talent around you, you might help develop some all-star performers, some organizational Olympians, some Denise Drapers.

Denise, with the help of family, coworkers, and others, turned her life experiences into the type of resolve that helped her thrive when she faced one of the toughest "stretch assignments" you could imagine a few years ago as an executive at a large bank.

After working her way up the corporate ladders in sales and marketing management in large corporations in different industries, Denise had moved home to Puerto Rico for a new job in the retail division of a large financial institution.

She arrived with no experience in the financial services industry, but she learned the ropes quickly and excelled in managing several products and projects. Then, after about two years with the bank, she got an unexpected offer. The senior vice president of the largest region of the bank, accounting for a significant percent of the company's net income—planned to retire. Denise's boss and mentor wanted to move her into that role.

"I thought he was crazy," Denise said of the decision.

But the man she would replace was staying on for another six months, her boss told her, which would provide an opportunity to transition into the new assignment. So two months later she reported to the job expecting to get four months of transition-training into the most challenging job of her career.

It didn't work out that way.

"I got in the office in December and he was gone," Denise told me. Instead of a soon-to-retire SVP who could show her the ropes, all she got was an empty desk. "I thought, 'That's no transition. I thought I had six months.'"

That was just the start of the surprises. Within three months, her top direct report—a man who had been passed over for her job—resigned and took a competing position at another bank.

"He got his bonus one morning and left that afternoon," she said. "And every week for eleven weeks he took one of my employees. It was the toughest time in my life. But it was also amazing."

Denise didn't respond with anger or frustration; she responded with a plan. The most important plan of her career.

"There was a large portfolio at risk," she said. "I said, 'I think the best strategy is to hire from the competing bank so they have to defend. Right now, we are defending and they are grabbing. We are only protecting.'"

With the support of her boss and other key executives at the bank, Denise got the resources she needed to take on the challenge and she and her mostly new team went to work. They worked long hours, called on clients relentlessly, went on the offensive, and ended up netting the portfolio millions more than their competitor that year.

"It was the hardest I'd ever worked and the most rewarding," Denise said.

Denise's boss and mentor saw something in her that told him to risk putting her in charge of an important division. He didn't know exactly what challenges she would face, but he knew she'd face challenges. And he knew her experiences would translate into the determination necessary to turn challenges into personal and professional victories. So he gave her a stretching assignment, and he also gave her the resources and backing she needed to succeed.

It wasn't that Denise developed resolve during her critical leadership crisis at the bank; the crisis exposed (and strengthened) her resolve. It was developed over the course of her career, sometimes at times when her talents were tapped and sometimes during times when she was figuring out how to tap into those talents.

The untapped talent in your organization most likely has reservoirs of resolve built from previous experiences in their lives—the times when they overcame obstacles, when they faced down a challenge, when they got back up after getting knocked down. For some, they just need a new challenge and someone who believes in them. Others need help rediscovering that talent or understanding how the resolve they once displayed can translate to the challenges they now face.

When you untap the resolve reservoir, everything changes. Your employees won't ever give up and they won't ever give in. They might not win every battle, but they'll always move themselves—and your organization—forward.

LEADERSHIP EXERCISE: CHECKING YOUR RESOLVE

Assess your resolve by completing the check list below. To put this in perspective, consider a situation when you were challenged with completing a project, or when you were passionate about an idea, or when you were unsuccessful and needed to turn a situation around. Think through all facets of the situation, the beginning when your energy may have been very high and things were working, the middle when unforeseen challenges developed and you had to draw on your reservoir of emotional energy, and the end when you crossed the finished line.

Resolve checklist	*Yes*	*Sometimes*	*No*
1. Do you view obstacles as challenges to be resolved?			
2. Do you learn from your mistakes and attempt to find new solutions and ways to approach a problem?			
3. Do you move forward when others advise you not to, or when a goal appears to be unobtainable?			
4. Do you show up even when you don't feel like it?			
5. Do you allow your passion to drive your progress forward?			
6. Do you remain on projects or assignments until they're completed?			
7. Do you maintain a balance between your physical and mental health when you're deeply involved in a project or assignment?			
8. Do you seek advice from others when you are at a stalemate?			
9. Do you believe that you are capable of succeeding in spite of every challenge life has to offer?			
10. Do you believe your confidence and resolve are built on your past successes?			

If you can answer "yes" to seven of the ten questions, chances are you have a strong ability to tap into your reservoir of resolve and move through challenging and difficult situations. If you were consistently answering "sometimes," you may experience what I call situational resolve—you push forward when required but waver at times. If you were answering "yes" to fewer than six questions, it's time you rethink how you feel about commitment, because commitment is the time between the past and the walk into the future.

For an in-depth analysis of your and your team's resolve, you can take the extended survey on resilience, resourcefulness, and resolve by going to www.centerfocus.com.

CHAPTER 12

Tapped Talent: Putting Purpose on the Right Path

This page intentionally left blank

> Leadership is the capacity to translate vision into reality.
> —Warren G. Bennis

If there's one thing that summarizes what you need to seek, engage, and ultimately set free the untapped talent in your organization, it is this: Vision.

Creating and living a powerful vision about "tapped talent" will fuel your passion for developing untapped talent. Your passion will infect the organization in a positive way. Your passion becomes their passion. Your vision becomes their vision.

To do that, your vision needs to connect to purpose, or what I call "operating from purpose." And when that happens—when you've created a vision grounded in purpose that inspires passion—you and the people around you end up on the right path, the path that frees untapped talent so that they can live and work at their ultimate potential.

What's the right path?

Earlier I referenced the ASTD's description of effective talent management: "[P]utting the right employee with the right skills in the right position at the right time." When all the "rights" are adding up, people are on the right path, but the "right" that's missing in that ASTD description is "right purpose." If people aren't operating from purpose—the right purpose for them—then some or all of their talents will go untapped and they'll get stuck in the hidden workforce.

Operating from purpose is how we bring our whole self to the job in a way that drives results. It's like having an internal compass that keeps us on track and aligns our energy, focus, and behaviors in the right direction; it puts us on the right path.

When people aren't operating from purpose, they're withholding parts of who they are while they are at work, and, therefore, they aren't engaging their full energy and passions in pursuit of maximum results. Remember Darla, the woman I referenced earlier who was hiding in plain sight? She wasn't operating from purpose. She was working without key parts of herself. Some of her talents were untapped. And it showed in her results.

Gays and lesbians have frequently shared with me that they have to change pronouns in the workplace when talking about their life partners in order not be discriminated against or judged. So the "hes" become "shes" (or vice versa) in their sentences, and covering up who they really are becomes a full-time job, taking away from their other full-time jobs. That's energy that should be used to produce results.

When we are operating from purpose and on the right path, work unfolds in a very synergistic way. It's as if we only have to ask for a solution to a situation and the solution appears or the right equipment or leader shows up—just in time. There's a flow to our work and life; it's not always effortlessness, but we find a certain peace in delivering high-performing results.

Consider how this has played out in the amazing story of William Kamkwamba. Growing up with his mom, dad, and six sisters on his family's small farm in Malawi, William dreamed of going to school and getting an education. After finishing the eighth grade, he was accepted into a secondary school. But in 2001–2002, a severe famine struck his country, and William's family no longer could afford the $80 for his annual school fees. So at 14, discouraged but not defeated, William began borrowing books from a small community library and studying on his own.

After flipping through *Using Energy*, an eighth-grade American textbook, he decided to build a windmill to bring electricity to his family's home. He found parts wherever he could—a broken bicycle, a fan blade from a tractor, old shock absorbers...He built a prototype, then a five-meter windmill that powered four light bulbs in his home, and then a twelve-meter model. His projects attracted attention from miles around, leading to news stories that inspired people to help him get back in school.

It took five years, but he returned to school and by 2010 he was enrolled at Dartmouth. His story, chronicled in *The Boy Who Harnessed the Wind*, which William wrote with Bryan Mealer, shows how a passion-inspired vision took William from the depths of despair and put him on a path to hope.

To untap his talents, Williams had to operate from purpose.

Kevin Cashman, author of *Leadership from the Inside Out*, defines that type of "core purpose" as "the high performance intersection where our talents and our values come together. It is the value-creating, catalytic moment when our gifts make a difference. When we split off our values from our talents, or vice versa, we compromise purpose...and enduring performance."[1]

William valued his education. He valued his creativity. He valued his ingenuity. And by operating from purpose based on those values and his talents, he harnessed the wind.

People on the right path—those, like William, who are operating from purpose—often make their work look easy and can accomplish things where others fail. For instance, a medical doctor I'll call Antonio was put in charge of expanding his organization's influence on health care in Africa by creating intern programs for local scientists. He was told it would take years to advance the organization's agenda in Africa, but Antonio, a dedicated and result-oriented person with a big heart, designed and implemented the first phase for internships in four months.

When I met him, he was preparing for the second class of interns. As he shared his story, I knew he was on the right path. His outside-the-box recommendations involved importing experts in medical research from countries where they were in abundance to Africa, where there was a shortage. He opened doors that were previously closed, and he worked with scientists to help them learn how to train scientists with lesser skills. He helped the mentors get through their unconscious bias around the local scientists' skills by coaching them about the backgrounds of their mentees. Antonio appreciated the difficulties that the local scientists faced—studying with limited resources and a lack of quality equipment. He was able to help the mentors recognize that challenging circumstances didn't equate to low aptitude.

Antonio could have practiced medicine or worked in a research lab, but he tapped into his core purpose—helping the less fortunate learn better medical research practices so they could improve the health of their citizens. Getting on this path and tapping into this purpose created energy; enthusiasm for his work radiated around him, and it generated tremendous results. It not only generated the results related to his organization's stated goals, but Antonio found himself experiencing real joy and satisfaction in his work. Like William, his "work" came to him as naturally and effortlessly as breathing.

Mihaly Csikszentmihalyi, well-known for his research and writing on happiness and creativity, calls it in "flow" or in "optimal experience." When we're in "flow," he says, it's as if we lose self-consciousness. "We may lose track of time, not even realizing how long and how hard we are working," he says. "The experience is so enjoyable we would do it even if we didn't have to. At the end of a day, although we may be tired, we don't feel drained. Instead, we feel a strong inner sense of fulfillment, and we look forward to the next day with eager anticipation."[2]

Flow becomes fun and fun becomes flow. Why? Energies are unblocked and we are using all our skills and talents, plus learning new ones. Our minds expand and our mental models are being recreated; we are experiencing a transformation, a paradigm shift in our work, in our minds, and in our bodies. All of a sudden, all the good things we considered about ourselves come to reality and, in doing so, we become someone new. Transformation takes place not from ego, but from standing and living our purpose.

Recognizing when we're operating from purpose and on the right path is not always easy. Purpose hides in the context of our daily lives. It's the "what we do" when we grow up, not the "how." The "what" is about the jobs, the positions, and the opportunities that come our way. The "what" is the title—doctor, lawyer, entertainer, football player, teacher, minister, or business person. The "how" is usually based on our core values and manifests in the work we choose. The "how" allows us to bring our whole selves into our work—our values, beliefs, expectations, worldview, and inner callings. "How" is the way we show up in our work.

Discovering our core purpose can involve reviewing all the positions, volunteer assignments, internships and events, exercises, situations, and people that bring us joy, as well as those that have caused great difficulty. It's the hard work of becoming, as we discussed earlier, "personally sound."

Pause a moment and ask yourself: When and how have I found meaning in life? What were the core principles that were operating? What skills and talents did I exercise or learn? Did I feel fulfilled? What encouraged my sense of fullness? Was my energy abundant? Was I connected to something greater than myself?

Your answers may not come easily, but I promise they will be revealing.

Over the years, I have visited these questions many times. My answers, while not surprising, were always informative. My purpose is to teach and bring awareness of inequities and the reality that we are all waiting to be tapped talent. I have reinvented myself many times to live my purpose. The context of my life has been lived through working as a counselor in community-based programs; as an administrator at a small junior college; teaching in an urban high school for at-risk teenagers; consulting and working in large, global corporations and organizations; and now by sharing the things I've learned with a larger audience as an author. Each assignment taught me how to "be" in my work. The daily job requirements and tasks held the structure for me to simply operate in purpose.

The Path to Vision

Passion, purpose, and path come together to form vision—your vision for your work, your vision for creating a culture of talent stewardship, and the vision you inspire in others who are ready to break free from the hidden workforce and make the most of their talents.

In all of those cases, for your vision to really matter, it has to really matter. In other words, your vision can't be some routine, lifeless platitude that inspires no one, least of all yourself. It has to inspire something in you and in others: Passion, purpose, path. They all feed each other.

Are you inspired by your vision? Is it a vision that inspires others, one they can share with tremendous energy? Does it inspire others to hold a powerful vision of their own?

Turning untapped talent into tapped talent requires that we ignite the fire within the people on our teams. We have to determine what gets them excited, what gets their juices flowing, and provide them with the opportunities to get on the right path and work from purpose.

This type of vision casting isn't a microwavable process. It takes time and effort, and sometimes it makes a bit of a mess.

Corporate vision statements came into vogue in the 1980s, and organizations around the world invested time and energy carefully crafting the wording that would describe their "ideal future states." Many of them held off-site retreats and included input from a diagonal slice of the organization, from the CEO down to the front-line supervisors. People debated, grew tired, reenergized themselves, fought, laughed, sometimes cried, and ultimately wordsmithed a draft that mattered. Then they sent it cascading around the organization for further massaging and tweaking. After several months of work, a vision was born. Colleagues committed to the vision, and change began to happen as the organization fused around the new direction.

Oh for the good old days.

Our fast-paced culture no longer allows for such a messy but productive process. Instead, an executive leadership team crafts a vision statement and sends it around the organization through a launch process. Leaders ferret out how their work connects to the vision, and then they sell that vision to their staffs. This streamlined process loses the key ingredients of energy and passion. It misses the core purpose. It can lead people down the wrong path, or, at minimum, a delayed journey.

Creating and living a vision for identifying, tapping into, and inspiring the untapped talent around you begins by removing all your blinders and starting with a clean slate. Incorporate the all-inclusive attitudes and behaviors of the 1980s, and let your imagination fly. See yourself differently. See your staff working differently. And certainly see how your organization works completely differently.

Envision a talent environment in which anything is possible—an ideal state.

Set your imagination free.

Imagine a workplace where people experience total self-expression. Their talents are recognized and applied to solve all sorts of challenges and problems. Because their voices are heard at conference tables around the world great ideas are formed and implemented. True collaboration, the fusing of differing opinions with the suspension of judgment, allows everyone to speak candidly but with respect.

Imagine a workplace where corporate entrepreneurship is rewarded and encouraged.

Imagine a workplace where your collegiate pedigree isn't the only indication of your aptitude or ability to have an impact, because the path you took to develop as a leader is less important than the leadership skills you developed on your unique path.

Imagine a workplace where you, as the leader, coach, sponsor, collaborate, and develop talent on your team and where two or three levels down you discover answers to complex business solutions because varying perspectives and diversity of thought have been allowed to emerge.

Imagine your organization's productivity increasing by 5, 10, or 15 percent, where engagement scores are high and where turnover is low because of the company's commitment to social responsibility.

Imagine a workplace where people go through the day with expressions of enthusiasm on their faces because they have the opportunity to succeed, where their strengths are based on their passions, and their passions develop their curiosity, and their curiosity leads to breakthroughs, and so on

What would be different about such work environments?

We would be tapping talent.

That's the vision. Make it your reality!

This page intentionally left blank

Notes

Introduction

1. Price Cobbs and William H. Grier, *Black Rage* (San Francisco, CA: Basic Books, 1968).

1 The Hidden Workforce

1. GDP for BRIC markets was above 7 percent for 2006–2008, while it hovered around 2 percent for G-7 markets, according to Standard &Poors.
2. Kate Linebaugh and James R. Hagerty, "Business Abroad Drives U.S. Profits," *Wall Street Journal*, B1, July 25, 2011.
3. Gocke Sargut and Rita Gunther McGrath, "Learning to Live with Complexity," *Harvard Business Review*, September 2011.
4. "The War for Talent" Organization and Leadership Practice, McKinsey & Company, April 2001.
5. "An Economy That Works: Job Creation and America's Future," McKinsey Global Institute, June 2011.
6. Jennifer Robison, "Despite the Downturn, Employees Remain Engaged," *GALLUP Management Journal*, January 14, 2010.
7. Rex W. Huppke, "Incorporating Happiness into the Workplace," chicagotribune.com, January 1, 2012.
8. "Employee Engagement: A Leading Indicator of Financial Performance," www.gallup.com/consulting/52/employee-engagement.aspx/ (referenced July 11, 2012).
9. Daniel Pink, *Drive: The Surprising Science of What Motivates Us* (New York: Penguin USA, 2009).
10. Gareth Cook, "The Dark Side of Happiness," *The Boston Globe*, October 16, 2011.
11. Some prominent researchers on this topic include June Gruber (Yale), Shawn Achor (Harvard), Martin Seligman (University of Pennsylvania, often called

the "father of positive psychology"), and Barbara Fredrickson (University of North Carolina).

2   Why Talent Goes Untapped

1. The assessment was a two-phase process that was comprised of an internal labor market analysis and focus groups. The internal labor market analysis identified the choke points (glass-ceiling) in an organization for women, blacks, Latinos, and Asians. It also explored the difference between buying or growing talent. Focus groups were used to collect qualitative data, in this case on women's experience in working in the organization on what supported their advancement and development or barriers that prevented advancement and development.
2. Malcom Gladwell, *Blink: The Power of Thinking without Thinking* (New York: Bay Books, 2005), pp. 86–87.
3. Laura Petrecca, "Number of Female 'Fortune' 500 CEOs at Record High," *USA Today,* October 26, 2011, http://www.usatoday.com/money/companies/management/story/2011–10–26/women-ceos-fortune-500-companies/50933224/1.
4. African American CEO's of Fortune 500 Companies, blackentrepreneurprofile.com, http://www.blackentrepreneurprofile.com/fortune-500-ceos/.
5. Madeline E. Heilman and Melanie H. Stopeck, "Being Attractive, Advantage or Disadvantage? Performance-Based Evaluations and Recommended Personnel Actions as a Function of Appearance, Sex, and Job Type," New York University, http://www.sciencedirect.com/science/article/pii/0749597885900354.

3   Blame the Brain

1. Shankar Vedantam, *The Hidden Brain* (New York: Spiegel & Grau, 2010), p. 7.
2. Ibid.,p. 33.
3. Ibid., p. 63.
4. John Powell and Rachel Godsil, "Implicit Bias Insights as Preconditions to Structural Change," *Poverty & Race* (September/October 2011), V20N5.
5. Vedantam, *The Hidden Brain*, p. 5.

4   Organizational Change: Tapping the 70 Percent

1. Lisa Vollmer, "Create Candor in the Workplace, Says Jack Welch," Stanford Graduate School of Business, April 1, 2005, http://www.gsb.stanford.edu/news/headlines/vftt_welch.shtml.

2. Karen Wilhelm Buckley and Dani Monroe, "Managing the Complexity of Organizational Transformation," in *Transforming Work*, edited by John D. Adams (Alexandria, Virginia: Miles River Press, 1988), p. 71.
3. Tom Peters and Robert H. Waterman, *In Search of Excellence, Lessons from America's Best Run Companies* (New York: Harper Collins, 1982).
4. www.freedomhouse.com/about.html.
5. I changed a few details about John's story, including his name, to protect his identity, but this illustration is based on a real person.
6. Thomas H. Stanton, *Why Some Firms Thrive While Others Fail: Government and Management Lessons from the Crisis* (New York: Oxford University Press USA, 2012).

5   The Culture Catapult

1. "The New Face of Talent Management," American Society of Training & Development (ASTD), 2009.
2. Ibid.
3. Nakiye Boyacigiller, Richard Goodman, and Margaret Phillips, eds., *Crossing Cultures: Insights from Master Teachers* (Blackwell Publishing, 2004).
4. Gary Wolf, "Steve Jobs: The Next Insanely Great Thing," *Wired*, February 1996; http://www.wired.com/wired/archive/4.02/jobs_pr.html.
5. "Collaboration Is Vital as Diversity of Thought Creates Excellence: Administrator of NASA," http://www.youtube.com/watch?v=qK5-jEfh8SE&feature=youtu.be(published August 21, 2012 by IBMIBV).
6. Scott Anthony, *The Little Black Book of Innovation: How It Works, How to Do It* (Boston: Harvard Business Press, 2012).
7. Scott Anthony, "How Do You Create a Culture of Innovation," www.fastcodesign.com/1669657/how-do-you-create-a-culture-of-innovation (accessed July 18, 2012).
8. Deloitte Research—It's 2008: Do You Know Where Your Talent Is? 2004.
9. Adrian Gostick and Chester Elton, "What the World's Best Cultures Look and Feel Like," *The Culture Works*, Issue #3, May 2012.

6   The Serendipitous Soft Skills of Tapped Talent

1. "Are They Really Ready to Work? Employers' Perspectives on the Basic Knowledge and Applied Skills of New Entrants to the 21st Century U.S. Workforce (2006)," The Conference Board, Corporate Voices for Working Families, the Partnership for 21st Century Skills, and the Society for Human Resource Management.
2. http://millennialbranding.com/2012/05/millennial-branding-student-employment-gap-study/ (accessed July 25, 2012).

3. Karen D. Arnold, "Academic Achievement—A View from the Top. The Illinois Valedictorian Project," North Central Regional Educational Laboratory, 1993.

7 Personally Sound: Tapping into Your Talents

1. J. Evelyn Orr, Victoria V. Swisher, King Yii Tang, and Kenneth P. De Meuse, "Illuminating Blind Spots and Hidden Strengths," The Korn/Ferry Institute, October 2010.
2. I changed the name to protect my friend's privacy.

8 The Three Rs: Emerging from the Hidden Workforce

1. Bob Johansen, *Leaders Make the Future: Ten Leadership Skills for an Uncertain World* (San Francisco: Berrett-Koehler Publishers, 2012).

9 Seeing Solutions: The Role of Resourcefulness

1. http://paulgraham.com/relres.html.

10 Failing Forward: The Role of Resilience

1. Lynn Harland, Wayne Harrison, James R. Jones, and Roni Reiter-Palmon, "Leadership Behaviors and Subordinate Resilience," *Journal of Leadership & Organizational Studies* vol. 11, no. 2 (Winter 2005).
2. Ibid.
3. The Road to Resilience, www.apa.org/helpcenter/road-resilience.aspx#.
4. Ibid.

11 Standing Firm: The Role of Resolve

1. Vahe Gregorian, "Blade Runner Inspires the Crowd by Finishing Second in 400-Meter Heat," *St. Louis Post-Dispatch*, August 5, 2012; http://www.stltoday.com/sports/olympics/blade-runner-inspires-the-crowd-by-finishing-second-in-/article_c28d354f-ed2b-5449-a888–2ba1c5d3ade7.html.

12 Tapped Talent: Putting Purpose on the Right Path

1. Kevin Cashman, *Leadership from the Inside Out: Becoming a Leader for Life* (San Francisco: Berrett-Koehler Publishers, 2008), p. 61.
2. Ibid., p. 62.

Index

Abdul-Aleem, Zaid, 121, 134–37
access, 31–33, 132–33
Adams, Alter, 48
Adidas, 16
All In (Gostick and Elton), 81
ambition, 90, 95, 120, 122
American Psychological Association (APA), 149
American Society for Training & Development (ASTD), 69, 165
Angalakudati, Mallik, 103–6, 111
Anthony, Scott, 80
Arnold, Karen, 88
assumptions
  see unconscious bias
Auguste, Donna, 80

Bakken, Jill, 34
Banaji, Mahzarin, 45–46
Bell Atlantic, 90, 93
Bennis, Warren G., 165
Bergson, Henri L., 59
Black Enterprise (Cobbs), 4
Black Rage (Cobbs and Grier), 3
Blink (Gladwell), 37
Block, Lawrence, 87
Bolden, Charles, 78
Bowman, Bob, 148
Boy Who Harnessed the Wind, The (Kamkwamba and Mealer), 167

Boyle, Susan, 20–21, 38
BRIC countries (Brazil, Russia, India, China), 16
Broken Window theory, 47
Budd, Wayne, 89–94

Carlin, George, 3
Carter, Jimmy, 38
Cashman, Kevin, 167
Center Focus International, Inc. (CFI), 50
Churchill, Winston, 153
Cobbs, Price, 3–5
cognitive fluency, 48
connecting the dots, 132
credibility, 93–94, 98
crucible experiences
  example, 107–8
  explained, 107
  identifying, 103
  leadership exercise, 114
  retrospective view of, 110–13
Csikszentmihalyi, Mihaly, 168
cultural competence, 17, 47, 88, 92, 96

Dittmer, Tom, 136
Dr. Seuss, 101
Draper, Denise, 121, 153–55, 159

E + E + E cultures, 81–82
Eastman Gelatine, 39–40
"Economics of Well-Being, The" (Kirby), 23
Elder, Mary, 141
Elton, Chester, 81
emotional intelligence, 63, 88, 91–92, 97
emphasizing investments, 131
entrepreneurship, 19, 80, 107, 154, 170
executive presence, 88, 92, 98
expertise, growing, 133

fears, facing, 132
Felix, Allyson, 159
Finkelstein, Sydney, 66
Fiorina, Carly, 119
Fitch, Ellen, 35
Flowers, Vonetta, 34–35
Fortune 500 companies, 15, 18, 37, 50

Gallup, 23–24
General Electric (GE), 16
Genzyme, 16
Gladwell, Malcolm, 37, 47
Godsil, Rachel, 51
Gostic, Adrian, 81
Greaux, Lisa Brooks, 72–73, 94
Grier, William H., 3
Gruber, June, 25
Gunther McGrath, Rita, 17

Hasbro, 16
heuristics, 47
Hidden Brain, The (Vedantam), 46, 51
hidden workforce
  defining, 20–21
  examples of, 21–23
  leadership exercise, 26
high-performance teams, 76–78, 166
homosexuality, 166

Implicit Association Test (IAT), 46, 53
In Search of Excellence, Lessons from America's Best Companies (Peters and Waterman), 61
Intercultural Productions, 50
interpersonal/external change, 63–65
interpersonal skills, 88, 92, 97–98

Jefferson, Cord, 112
Jobs, Steve, 8, 77
Johansen, Bob, 119–20
John Hancock Financial, 16, 90, 93
Jordan, Michael, 130

Kamkwamba, William, 166–68
Kelling, George, 47
Kirby, Julia, 23
Kotter, John, 60

Lawler, Edward, 78
Leaders Make the Future (Johansen), 119
leadership ability, 88, 92, 98, 109
leadership exercises
  assessing your hidden workforce, 26
  assessing your talent culture, 83
  charting resourcefulness, 138
  checking your resolve, 162
  crucible experiences, 114
  reducing unconscious bias, 53–54
  setting your path, 9
  taking soft skills inventory, 96–98
  untapped quiz, 41–42
Leadership from the Inside Out (Cash), 167
"Leading through Connections" study, 76–77
Lee, Michele, 74
Little Black Book of Innovation, The (Anthony), 80

Madison, James, 38
Manulife Financial, 16
Martin, Ralph, 90
Matthews, Chris, 63
McDonald's, 16
McKinsey & Company, 18–19
McKinsey 7-S model, 60
Mealer, Bryan, 167
Michaels, John, 64–65
Moneyball, 29

Obama, Barack, 17, 38–39
opening access, 132–33
Oppenheimer, Daniel, 48
Orbitz, 29
organizational change
   interpersonal/external, 63–65
   organizational, 65–66
   overview, 59–61
   personal/internal, 61–63
Owings, Suzanne, 4

Pacific Management Systems, 3
passion, 158–59, 165–67, 169–71
   identifying, 94–95
   purpose and, 165–67
   resolve and, 158–59, 162
   resourcefulness and, 130, 155
   untapped talent and, 8, 24–25
   vision and, 169–71
Pavarotti, Luciano, 130
peers, 63–65
personal/internal change, 61–63
Peters, Tom, 60
Phelps, Michael, 148, 159
physical appearance, 37–39
Pink, Daniel, 15
Pistorius, Oscar, 154–55, 159
political savvy, 88, 92, 97
Powell, John, 51

Reebok, 16
Reilly, Thomas, 89
resilience
   building, 147–49
   evaluating, 150
   example of, 142–47
   overview, 141–42
resolve
   committing to, 155–56
   face of, 159–61
   leadership exercise, 162
   overview, 153–55
   passion and, 158–59
   process of, 159
   pushing hard/pushing back, 158
   success/failure and, 156–58
resourcefulness
   day-to-day, 130
   face of, 133–37
   leadership exercise, 138
   overview, 127–29
   tapping into, 130–31
   tapping into your networks, 132–33
   tapping into yourself, 131–32
rewards, 73, 81–82, 170
"River of Life," 103–7
Robison, Jennifer, 23
rules, teaching, 131–32

Sam's Club, 71
Samuels, Mark, 48–49
Sanofi-Aventis, 16
Sargut, Gocke, 17
Schein, Edgar, 71
self-awareness
   crucible experiences, 110
   discovery and, 101–2
   happiness and, 25
   as soft skill, 88, 92, 95–96
self-preservation, 46–47
setting your path, 9–10

skills gap, 18–20
Smithson, Anne, 121, 141–47
soft skills, 66, 75, 87–98, 120
   developing, 60, 66, 75, 93–95
   emotional intelligence and, 63
   knowledge and, 92–93
   leadership exercise, 96–98
   overview, 87–88
   spotting, 91–92
   taking inventory of, 96
   Wayne Budd and, 89–91
Stanton, Thomas, 66
Strangfeld, John R., 69

talent stewardship, culture of
   assumptions and, 79–80
   leadership exercise, 83
   new opportunities and stretch assignments, 81
   nonmonetary rewards and, 81–82
   nontraditional approach with high-performance teams, 76–78
   overview, 70–73
   search for talent, 78–79
   understanding talent within organization, 73–76
Thurman, Howard, 25, 95
Tipping Point, The (Gladwell), 47
Toomer, Jean, 127
touch points, 15

unconscious bias, 45–54
   becoming aware of, 79
   Broken Window theory and, 47
   crucible experiences and, 109
   examples, 49–51
   experience and, 47–48
   leadership exercise, 53–54
   overview, 45–46
   poor decisions and, 66
   self-preservation and, 46–47
   understanding, 51–52
   untapped talent and, 7, 70, 167
United Technologies, 16
untapped talent
   employees don't have "traditional" look, 36–39
   failure to see uses for person's skills, 34–35
   lack of a "fit" and, 33–34
   lack of access and, 30–32
   lack of inclusion, 39–40
   lack of preparedness for opportunity, 35–36
   leadership exercise, 41–42
   navigating, 9–10
   overview, 29–30
   redundancy of, 40

Vedantam, Shankar, 46, 51
Verizon, 93
vision, path to, 169–71

Waterman, Robert H., 60
Welch, Jack, 59
Why Some Firms Thrive While Others Fail (Stanton), 66
Wiley, Fletcher, 90
Wilhelm Buckley, Karen, 60
Wilson, James Q., 47
Wilson, Leon, 62
Wisdom Connection, 60
Wright, Orville, 45
Wright, Steven, 90

GPSR Compliance

The European Union's (EU) General Product Safety Regulation (GPSR) is a set of rules that requires consumer products to be safe and our obligations to ensure this.

If you have any concerns about our products, you can contact us on

ProductSafety@springernature.com

In case Publisher is established outside the EU, the EU authorized representative is:

Springer Nature Customer Service Center GmbH
Europaplatz 3
69115 Heidelberg, Germany